Roar
of thunder
Whisper
of wind

PHOTOGRAPHS BY C.J. ELFONT · TEXT BY EDNA A. ELFONT

TwoPeninsula Press · Lansing, Michigan · 1984

PUBLISHER: Russell McKee
EDITORS: Janice E. Kreider,
   Richard Morscheck, Susan Newhof Pyle
ART DIRECTOR: Gijsbert van Frankenhuyzen
BOOK DESIGN: Leianne F Wright
GRAPHICS ASSISTANT: Joe Sienkiel
HAND LETTERING: Ron Bell Design, Lansing
DUOTONES: Modern Litho, Grand Rapids
PRINTING: The John Henry Company, Lansing
BINDING: John H. Dekker & Sons, Grand Rapids
PAPER: 70-pound Black and White Gloss by the
   Mead Corporation, Escanaba
TYPE: Text in 11/13 Garamond Light

*Roar of Thunder, Whisper of Wind—A Portrait
of Michigan Waterfalls* is Volume V of the
Michigan Heritage Series, and is a publication of
TwoPeninsula Press, a unit of

NATURAL RESOURCES MAGAZINE

Box 30034, Lansing, MI 48909

Detail of Au Train Falls

PREFACE

Four years ago, the Michigan Natural Resources Magazine program, a completely self-supporting "Enterprise Fund" that operates within the Michigan Department of Natural Resources, began to publish a series of fine quality books about Michigan—it's people and it's natural environment. Our purpose was to produce a ready-made Michigan reference library for the home, school, and public library. We called it our Michigan Heritage series because we wanted these books to provide all of us with a strong bond to our past so that we will be able to share that legacy with all generations to come. The first four books that we've published to date have all received a very warm reception, from the critic as well as from the fireside reader. Two of the books in fact, have been honored with special awards for outstanding graphic design and printing excellence. This book, the fifth volume in the series, carries on that tradition. We are especially proud that this book is the first major work ever published on the waterfalls of Michigan. We know it will serve you well as a guidebook, and we have included a special booklet that will assist you on your own waterfall adventures. Additionally, we believe that this book is also a very fine art book that responds to the renewed interest in black and white photography as an artform and as a means of creative expression. In this context, we're certain that photography enthusiasts will appreciate the technical notes found in the back of the book. But whether you've chosen this book as a guidebook or as an art book, we certainly hope that you will enjoy it, and that you will share it with others in the years ahead.

Richard Morscheck
May, 1984

DEDICATION

*For our daughter, Dayna and the generations that follow.
May they have the opportunity to personally experience that
which we have put on these pages.*

ACKNOWLEDGEMENTS

We owe a debt of gratitude to a number of people who contributed to the completion of this book. We extend special thanks to Jane Elder, without whom this whole project might never have begun. Our sincere appreciation for encouragement throughout the project goes to Richard Morscheck, managing editor of Michigan Natural Resources Magazine. We are grateful for the help of those who shared with us whatever information they could collect or recall. Among these are Irvin Kuehner and Bruce Vollmer of the Michigan Department of Natural Resources and Lawrence Lemanski of the Great Lakes Camp and Trail Association, Inc., who gave us the benefit of their personal knowledge and experience; Clarence Monette who sent us a selection of newspaper articles about Ontonagon and Baraga county waterfalls; Margaret LaMothe of the Alger County Chamber of Commerce, who shared her coffee and kitchen, as well as her information; Dr. H. Crum of the University of Michigan Herbarium who defined the nature of the moss at Scott Falls for us; Leroy Stevens, a recently retired forester, who accompanied us to, and informed us about, Sturgeon River Gorge and Canyon Falls; and Kevin Klotz, who guided us to the Black River falls and offered us the hospitality of his home. Our thanks, too, go to Mary Saflarski, who took us out of the rain and into her home. We must also recognize our niece, Amy Orlick for her companionship and assistance carrying camera gear on one of our trips, and our daughter, Dayna Elfont, who accompanied us on two other occasions. And we are especially grateful to the people of the Upper Peninsula, whose names we never knew, who either directed, informed, or befriended us on our journey in search of Michigan's waterfalls.

TABLE OF CONTENTS

I made what I knew would be the last entry in my journal and set it down to take a last look at the waterfall before me. The sun had just set and although this had to be the sixtieth waterfall C.J. and I had visited in Michigan (I had long since lost the exact count), we slowly and unenthusiastically packed our gear. During our waterfall search, our car had somehow accumulated some 5,000 miles and yet we had never felt travel weary. We had made four trips over the course of two years, and I surely expected by the end of our last trip to be grateful if I never saw a waterfall again. And yet, when I knew it was time to leave the last site, I did so reluctantly.

Historically, waterfalls have captured the attention of painters, photographers, poets and musicians alike. It is amazing that a simple thing like water falling over a rocky ledge can inspire so much emotional response. Webster's New Twentieth Century Dictionary defines a waterfall as "a steep fall of water from a height." Geologists go further to classify waterfalls into three main types: 1) those produced by physical changes in the level of a river bed due to faulting (vertical movement of the earth's crust) or glaciation; 2) those produced by differential erosion, which occurs when weak and resistant rock are juxtaposed in a river or stream bed; and 3) those that are attributable to deposits that form dams or barriers. Michigan's waterfalls are generally of the second type. Interesting as such information may be, it is certainly not the stuff of which poems and concertos are made! A waterfall is more than just the sum of its tangible parts. I could painstakingly list every physical attribute of a waterfall and still arrive at an incomplete description, for each fall has its own aura, giving it a uniquely individual character. To describe this character, some of the best words seem to be those used to describe the human personality such as powerful, tranquil, moody, charming, or enthusiastic. C.J. and I have found that only after the words, poems, images, and scientific data are put together, do we even begin to convey the real character of a waterfall.

It has always been difficult to explain why we have been so fascinated by water regardless of whether it is in oceans, lakes, rivers, or streams. We were both born and bred urbanites, C.J. growing up in Baltimore, Maryland, and I in Brooklyn, New York. Our only exposure to the "great outdoors," prior to our twenties, was summer camp. Perhaps our love of the outdoors was simply a response to our common childhood deprivation. In addition, sudden and dramatic mood changes seem to characterize any natural site of water. It is these mood changes that each of us has tried to capture and express in his own way. I have always felt that C.J.'s images of water show a special sensitivity for the intense, yet transient, spirit of such places. Perhaps it is the challenge to portray this mercurial spirit that continues to lure us.

After moving to Michigan in 1972, we began to anticipate great photographic possibilities when we learned some of Michigan's vital statistics. Not only does the state have more freshwater shoreline than any other state (3,251 miles to be exact), but there are 36,350 miles of inland streams and 2,000 miles of major rivers. Of Michigan's 35,000 mapped lakes and ponds which cover 841,000 acres, 15,800 cover two or more acres. The possibilities were enormous! When we subsequently discovered the dearth of photographic and written information concerning Michigan's scenery, we attempted to do something to partially correct the situation.

Our first extensive trip into Michigan's woods came when C.J. offered a Michigan outdoor group a trade. He would photograph whatever areas most interested them in return for a guided tour, some information, and help hauling our gear. When they saw some of his photographic images from our trips to Utah, Texas, California, and Colorado, they seemed anxious to get started. After poking about in the sand dunes lining the western shore of Michigan's Lower Peninsula, we headed for our first good look at the Upper Peninsula. We discovered that many inhabitants of the Lower Peninsula think of the Upper Peninsula in the same terms as they think of Alaska. Somehow they know it's "up there," and it's gorgeous, but it's "so far away." Actually, the Mackinac Bridge, which connects the Lower to the Upper Peninsula, is only 280 miles from Detroit, the southernmost large city in Michigan. Even if we had had to travel three times the distance, the trip would have been worth making because all across the Upper Peninsula were sites of scenic beauty secreted away like so many prizes at an Easter egg hunt. After roaming the magnificent lakes of the Sylvania Recreation Area in the southwest Upper Peninsula where we were treated to such sights as an eagle on a training flight with her fledgling, we were guided to our first Upper Peninsula waterfall. Expecting a pretty, but less than spectacular site, what we found at Sturgeon River Gorge Falls destroyed any preconceived notions we might have had. We found ourselves at the bottom of a 250-foot gorge with sculptured, red, sandstone walls. In the riverbed lay the blackened rock remains of an ancient lava flow, over which thundered a 40-foot falls. The second waterfall we visited was Rock River Falls, a beautiful bridal veil falls, which was totally secluded, and whose location was made even more obscure by dense vegetation. C.J. and I were entranced!

We wanted the chance to see more waterfalls, photograph and write about them as well. After inquiring, we were told that there were at least 150 named waterfalls in the Upper Peninsula. No one was even willing to venture a count of the unnamed falls. The number left us a bit open-mouthed, and suddenly it looked as if we had quite a project on our hands. First we needed information. I contacted the Upper Peninsula Tourist Bureau, anticipating a response that would make my mailman grimace. I certainly was not prepared for the one under-nourished pamphlet I received, which merely listed 119 falls and supplied only a name and a general location, using the fewest possible words. After checking out other information sources, I realized that so little information was available that we might as well have asked about top secret missile sites. Our curiosity was aroused. We had never seen an ugly waterfall, so we couldn't imagine why Michigan was hiding hers like so much old furniture. And so we began our waterfall search armed with a list of falls, a plethora of county maps, cameras, notebooks, high hopes, and vague plans. We never anticipated reaching as many falls as we did, but we were to discover that our curiosity was not easily satiated.

We found that the people of the Upper Peninsula constituted a resource as valuable as its natural beauty. They offered not only much-needed information and directions but frequently the hospitality of their homes as well. These are people who love their land and, some of them, may fear that visitors will bring noise, litter, and destruction. Perhaps my only hesitation in making our "discoveries" public, is that there may be some visitors who will prove them correct. I also hope, however, that as conservation awareness increases, the number of uncaring people will decrease to an insignificant number.

One need
Only see to
Know creation is not
Locked in the aging pages of
A book

Gabbro Falls

Clouds
of mist
in the
wilderness

WESTERN UPPER PENINSULA

GOGEBIC & ONTONAGON COUNTIES

ogebic, the Upper Peninsula's westernmost county, is separated from Wisconsin on its west by the Montreal River. It was on this river, during a May snowstorm, that we discovered Superior and Saxon Falls, two of Michigan's outstanding waterfalls. I had no idea what we would find that frigid day for all I had to go by was two groups of three little squiggles on the county map, each of which was supposed to indicate a waterfall. On occasion, in the past, we had found nothing more at the site of a "squiggle" than an old beaver dam, but this time our search was rewarded with a visual feast. After walking only 100 yards from an electric substation along a wooded path, we abruptly reached the edge of an outcropping and found ourselves at the top of a cliff overlooking a steep-walled gorge, approximately 100 to 150 feet deep. The river appeared from behind a stand of trees and made its way through a sharp, Z-shaped turn before thundering about 40 feet over a precipice in a single column of white foam. Superior is a formidable falls; as testimony to its raw power, billowing clouds of mist were rising high above the falls toward the cliff top where we stood.

This approximately 30-foot-wide falls comes quickly to rest in a large pool. From there the water creeps around both sides of a small, central, rocky island and meanders its way through the gorge into Lake Superior, which we could see off to our right. The amount of foam produced by the falls was so great during our visit that its white tendrils streamed through the river, persisting until they dissipated in the water of the great lake.

The fracture lines in the rock around the falls are almost vertical, which gave me the feeling that awesome forces deep in the earth must have caused a massive upheaval to tilt the rock at such an angle. Some areas of the gorge wall appeared free of vegetation and lighter in color than others—trademarks of recent rock slides. We speculated that in better weather it might be possible to hike upstream to the falls from Lake Superior. We could not determine, however, if a negotiable path existed, and the sheer rise of the gorge walls from the riverbed lessened the possibility of finding one. The light dusting of snow on the rocky ledges and the newly emerged buds made a magnificent backdrop for an impressive falls. Superior Falls definitely rates more than three little squiggles on a map!

Not far from a location sign for Saxon Falls, we encountered another electric substation where an employee of the power company directed us down a long flight of metal stairs. He told us there was a dam upstream not visible from this site. The unpredictable spring snow began to fall with even greater intensity just as we unloaded all the camera gear and started down the steps. We walked out onto a bridge which spanned the river, and there before us was one of the most majestic and spectacular falls either of us had ever seen!

The portion of Saxon Falls visible from the bridge is composed of three sections separated by towering, rocky pinnacles capped with pine trees. The pinnacles loomed out of the snowy mist like towers of some medieval castle, lending mystery and timelessness to the scene. The section of the falls on the left appeared to be the highest of the three, perhaps 30 to 35 feet, and it poured down in three foamy tiers. Before emptying into a wide pool, 80 to 90 feet across, the water of the lower tier rolled over a multi-faceted, dome-shaped rock, breaking the water into many tiny falls. The right section was the most powerful of the three, thundering over its precipice in a translucent sheet that transformed into white plumes when it encountered a rocky lower ledge. A column of fog and mist rose from behind the three falls creating a watercolor effect by softening the outlines of the trees and rock. Above this mist rose a pine forest dusted with snow. By climbing up a metal ladder which followed a pipeline on the far side of the gorge, I discovered that the source of the mist, visible from below, was a fourth, three-tiered waterfall, which hurtled in from above and behind the front three. It was at least as high as the others and poured forth, within one cataract, the same volume of water that divided below into three falls.

Although the pool below the lower three falls narrows where it meets the main riverbed, the river remains quite wide. We were content to stay on the bridge and not venture onto the riverbanks, for there were signs warning of sudden and dramatic changes in the water level caused by the opening of the dam gates just upstream. With so much potential power, Saxon Falls is not a swimming-in type of falls—it is a standing-by-and-admiring kind of falls that left us with a sense of wonder and discovery.

In at least one other spot in Gogebic County, the topography truly favors the waterfall seeker, for along the Black River we found five waterfalls within three miles of one another. The Black River runs 30 horizontal miles and drops 1000 vertical feet from its Wisconsin origin before it empties into Lake Superior. In the last three miles before reaching the lake, it forms Great Conglomerate Falls, Potawatomi Falls, Gorge Falls, Sandstone Falls, and Rainbow Falls.

We reached Potawatomi Falls after a short walk through a forest. The well-groomed trail ends in a set of wooden steps which lead to an observation platform. In late summer, water levels are low, leaving much of the interesting and sometimes beautiful rock exposed. Ours was an August visit, and the water above the falls ran through a fairly broad riverbed until it encountered a large, flat table-top of rock over which it spilled in two streams. Between the streams is a wedge of conglomerate rock, commonly called "puddingstone." Originally, this conglomerate was laid in flat beds intermixed with lava flows on top of the bedrock over which the river now runs. The riverbed was later tilted when the mountains of the Gogebic Range were formed. These have since been worn down by glaciers and other environmental forces, leaving only hills. The water now falls over a graded drop of 60 to 100 feet.

Returning to the road, we drove until we found a sign indicating Gorge Falls.

Following a short trail, we snacked on sweet, fuzzy thimbleberries which grew in profusion along the path. The trail ended at some steep wooden steps leading down to an observation platform at river level. The high, vertical walls of the gorge are composed of conglomerate rock and topped with imposing pines. Across from the observation deck, a small pine had gained a foothold on the gorge wall and was making a valiant effort to secure itself. The main portion of the straw-colored falls catapults through a narrow chasm and then plunges downward about 40 feet. There are cave-like depressions on both sides of the falls and the water has carved a crescent-shaped depression in the rock below.

Walking to our left before reaching the final group of stairs, we reached another platform facing away from the falls, which afforded a marvelous view of the narrow gorge and downstream area. The steep gorge walls border the river for a distance, and as we watched, foam produced by the force of the falls accumulated in quiet areas far downstream. The riverbanks are coated with shattered conglomerate rock which has been torn from the gorge walls and thrown about by the river's force.

In 1847 and 1848, William Burt, a government surveyor, wrote about a cavern below the falls and a nearby abandoned copper mine. He also described the area's use by the Chippewa Mining Company, one of many such companies which came looking for copper. The elusive metal was never found in more than trace amounts here, yet the area's aura of history was so strong, I almost expected the image of an 1840s miner to appear on C.J.'s film.

f the five Black River falls, Rainbow is the closest to Lake Superior and the least known, perhaps because it has not been well marked. The river trail we finally found led upstream to the falls and was bordered by a lush growth of ferns. We guessed that, in season, the mushroom growth would be prolific. The trail led along the top of a steep-walled gorge and ended in a series of steps from which we were able to reach the top of the falls. Rainbow Falls spills in two distinct streams over a rock shelf into a three-sided, rocky cistern, 40 feet below. Turning almost 90 degrees, the river emerges from the open side of the cistern and proceeds toward Lake Superior. This falls derived its name from the rainbows that form above it whenever the sun shines through the constant mist produced by, and rising over, the falls. The rainbows glow with an almost fluorescent gleam against the dark background of the rocky surroundings. Captivated, we stayed to watch the last rainbow fade as the deepening shadows all but obscured this lovely falls.

Another superb site in Gogebic County is Gabbro Falls, visited almost exclusively by the local residents. We had difficulty finding this falls, known to some nearby residents as Baker's Falls, but after making several inquiries we found ourselves hiking along a well-worn trail which began as a gradually graded

Superior Falls

path through tall grasses. The trail became more difficult to negotiate as we got closer to the falls and we had to engineer our way down a steep riverbank to get to water level. The edge of the riverbank was strewn with large boulders, upon which were the prone figures of several sunbathers. A massive rock wall decorated with mosses and ferns stretched across the width of the river.

Looking toward the west side of the river, a nearly 20-foot cascade of water is visible which, I later learned, is the last in a series of three such cascades. A large boulder splits the top of this third cascade in two. This segment of the falls is closely flanked on both sides by massive boulders, one of which is about 50 feet high. It was from this height that we watched some local swimmers leap into the small, deep pool below. From river level, it looked like a long way down and the size of the pool did not appear to allow much leeway for a jumper with poor aim. We watched some ten-year-olds jump without hesitation, while two eighteen-year-olds spent ten minutes apiece working up the courage to detach themselves from the rock. Perhaps there is a rule of physical science we've overlooked—the height of an object increases in direct proportion to the age of the observer!

The immense boulders that flank these falls are an unusual greenish-black, typical of the material geologists call gabbro rock. To my knowledge, this is the only Michigan falls that flows over this type of rock. Gabbro was formed by the cooling of a portion of magma as it was pushed into the earth's upper crust. Its color is partially caused by concentrations of augite and it is found in several locations in the western half of the Upper Peninsula. The very presence of gabbro rock evoked specters of the earth in transition! By late afternoon, the sun infused the western cascade with a golden glow and lit the foam as the falls tossed it up into the air. Clouds of mist rose off the water's surface through shafts of sunlight and drifted across the massive black boulders, giving this place an other-world appearance. My imagination could not dismiss the possibility that a "something-saurus" might suddenly appear from behind those rocks.

The water of a section of the falls to my immediate left was so delicate and filmy that it looked like falling snow. This section was in sharp contrast with the more westerly cascade. I was entranced, but the falls had not yet run out of visual treats. I suddenly realized that globs of "suds" were being flung into the air high above the falls from somewhere behind the rocks at the top. These white blobs of bubbles would then drift lazily earthward, coming to rest on the uppermost rocks. An endless stream of the sudsy projectiles continued skyward, but I was not to discover their source until later.

We went back out to the gravel road and followed it north until we found a bridge which crossed the river. Still not sure that Gabbro and Baker's Falls were two names for the same site, we stopped at a cabin along the road and spoke with a man working there. He informed us that Gabbro Falls was within rock throwing distance of where he stood and that he would gladly show us the way. He led us down a short path, through a dense growth of birch and pine, that came to an abrupt end at the top of a ledge. Below the ledge was another part of the falls we had missed. Surprisingly, the section of falls we saw from the west side of the river was not visible from the east, and sections we had seen from the east, were no longer in view. We maneuvered our way towards the falls along the ledge, taking great care, for the ledge is narrow and the drop from its edge is considerable. Peering over the edge, I saw a powerful 20- to 25-foot cascade which empties into a three-sided rock cistern. The water was roaring over its first ledge with so much power that foam was hurled out of the cistern and into the air, producing the flying suds I had seen earlier. Over the open side of the cistern, and at right angles to the first cascade, pours a second larger cataract, which falls another 25 to 35 feet. The water then proceeds over a third ledge, turned at right angles from the second, thus forming the cascade we had seen earlier from the east side, but now hidden from view. Gabbro Falls is really an intricate complex of rock and falls which have to be seen from both sides to be fully appreciated.

Two rainbows appeared through the heavy mist lending their own special splendor to an already imposing sight. In August, when we were there, the water flow was torrential, but we were told it is even greater during the spring run-off when clouds of mist may rise 200 feet in the air. The flow is so great, that even during the drier portions of the year, mosses can grow only near the areas of smallest water flow. As the light softened toward evening, the massive black gabbro boulders looked ominous as they became shrouded in mist.

Unlike our warm weather trip to Gabbro Falls, we visited Yondota Falls, about four miles north of Marenisco, on a cold day in May when the temperature hovered near freezing. We arrived in the late afternoon following a morning snowshower, and the young pines, along the short walk to the falls, still held a dusting of snow. At a spot where the noise of the falls was the loudest, we climbed out onto a large, rocky, wing-shaped promontory and found ourselves at the top of the falls. The river above makes a Z-shaped turn and then churns its way through a narrow chasm. In a single torrent, the falls then thunder over a V-shaped precipice which faces a steep cliff wall on the opposite bank. This makes the falls extremely difficult to see from downstream.

The river below the falls is 40 to 50 feet wide for quite a distance but the water's power is not quickly dissipated. It surges through the riverbed in golden billows, cartwheeling over all but the largest rocks to form an extensive series of rapids. Farther downstream, just below the point at which a small tributary joined the river, the flow slowed and the river sounds softened. The moss growth, which bordered much of the path, was elaborate. Different species grew together in such intricate patterns that the arrangements looked predetermined. We became fascinated by these mini-gardens and by the common mullein which grew in abundance. Equally intriguing were the trees, which had assumed strange shapes as if frozen in mid-step during some interpretive dance. The dark bands that wove free-form patterns through the otherwise light-toned rocks, completed the picture of a falls where motion and form was reflected in all its elements.

Kakabika Falls, about 14 miles west of Watersmeet, was the most easterly falls we visited in Gogebic County. Only a three-minute walk was necessary to reach the falls. The trail closely followed the river and led through a young and tranquil pine forest, dappled with sunlight. The river bounded past, bouncing through small rapids and cascades for much of the way. Soon we found ourselves at a small falls divided into two streams by a rocky hillock at its center. Atop the hillock were two pines, one of which had been uprooted, and another that still maintained a tenuous hold on the rock. Bordering this five-foot-high section of falls, was a large boulder with several young pines growing in the moss that crowned it. Just below this cascade, the river turned about 45 degrees away from us and narrowed considerably. In order to follow the river's edge, I had to climb to the top of a high, rocky rise. From this vantage point, I saw the level of the stream bed drop noticeably. The water plunged through a narrow channel, six to eight feet across, where it seemed to hit a ledge of submerged rock immediately behind a second falls. This caused the water to catapult upward in an unbroken white plume, obscuring the ledge over which it fell. Most of the rock was submerged and there was no quiet pool. As if to contrast with the waters' vigorous flow, the banks of the stream bed were carpeted with moss and with fern, giving them a garden-like appearance. Some of the pines extend their branches over the top of the falls as if attempting to slow the waters' hasty passage. We stayed late into the day and watched the setting sun replace all the vibrant hues with a colorful array of soft and dusty pastels.

orthwest of Kakabika Falls, on the Presque Isle River and within the boundries of the Porcupine Mountains Wilderness State Park, are a number of waterfalls of which four are in Gogebic County: Manido, Manabezho, Nawadaha, and Iagoo Falls. Of these four, we visited the first two, for they were the most accessible. Also in this region, but not within the park's limits, are Nokomis, Abinodji, Ogima, and Ogimakwe Falls. Manido Falls, the smaller of the two we saw, was forceful enough to command respect but not so high as to be overwhelming. In the winter, we were told, the surface of the falls freezes but the roaring of the water beneath can still be heard. During our August visit, Manido Falls spanned the 125-foot width of the river and its multiple cascades plunged over a 12-foot, sculptured, black slate ledge. There was one large rock at the center of the falls, around which the water stormed with only small rivulets running over its face, causing it to resemble a city park fountain. The falls are flanked on one side by a large, low, wing-shaped rock ledge into which the water has carved hills and

Manabezho Falls

valleys. On the other side, the falls have deeply undercut the rock at its base, forming a protruding shelf below which is a dark, cave-like depression. The clear, cold water made wading irresistible.

Just downstream from Manido Falls, the water momentarily quieted, then quickly gained speed and roared over a nearly 30-foot ledge to form Manabezho Falls. Here, columns of falling water alternated with protruding rocky pillars. The falling water looked like blond hair blowing in the wind. This broad, powerful falls of approximately 200 feet in width generates a prodigious amount of spray and foam. The steep cliff wall surrounding the falls was adorned with several varieties of fern, moss, and lichen, and was ornately decorated with chiseled stone columns. Sitting beneath these columns in the cooling spray of the falls, contentment truly reigned.

Of the six Porcupine Mountains Wilderness State Park falls shown on the map as being within Ontonagon County, only Union and Greenstone Falls were easily accessible. Union Falls is within a few long strides of a pleasant campground but it is really more of a rapids than a falls. According to our map, Greenstone Falls should have been about a mile from where we'd have to leave our car if we followed the trail through the forest. We followed the river, however, for it looked like a shorter walk, and we thought it might be more photographically interesting. We walked no more than two minutes and found ourselves at a falls. Nothing on our maps indicated its presence, so we named it Overlooked Falls. Overlooked is delightful and charming—the kind of falls that, if it could speak, would do so with a lilt in its voice. This small, six-foot-high falls has two main sections. One section bubbled out from under the large, toppled trunk of a pine tree and fell over a centrally placed rock as a many-tiered cascade. The other section poured over its ledge as a single, sliding cascade of surprising force. As it fell, this section bounced off submerged rocks sending fingers of foam skyward. The water patterns of the tiered section looked like those of a well-planned fountain, and its misty flow would have been the perfect backdrop for a romantic movie scene. On the rocks between the two portions of the falls was a small pine just gaining a foothold on life by growing on what little soil clung to the rock's surface. Downstream were two, small cascades stacked one above the other; the first with a large rock at its center and the second with a ledge so smooth and regular that it appeared handmade. The wading looked superb.

Surrounding these falls is an imposing pine forest standing on a thick pad of vivid green moss. Perched on one such padded rock, I decided that Overlooked Falls was definitely a sitting-by-and-thinking type of falls, the kind from which you come away feeling pleasant and refreshed. Here, even a casual traveler can sample the flavor of this superb country.

Reaching Greenstone Falls required a bit more effort, but in good weather it's a pleasant walk through a pine forest. Mushrooms abound and we found the feeling of isolation in the woods intense, yet comforting. Located within a stone's throw of a frontier cabin, Greenstone is a small but vigorous falls, racing its way under a dead tree trunk and falling five to six feet in bunches of tiny cascades. As it hurries through a deep, wide pool, just made for a summer afternoon swim, it leaves an arc of white foam. A sandy shelf protrudes into the river from shore, making it possible to sit right next to the falling water. This is a small, quiet falls, but well worth the effort needed to find it.

onesuch Falls is located on the Little Iron River, just outside the Porcupine Mountains Wilderness State Park, so it didn't appear on the park maps. We arrived in early May, after a very snowy winter and a wet spring, so we were not surprised that we could drive only half the length of the road before it turned into water holes and mud. The entire length of the road is less than half-a-mile long, so walking even its full length would present few problems. Skirting the swampier areas, we followed the road through a grassy field surrounded by yellow birch—one of the loveliest stands we had ever encountered. We passed the remains of an old wooden cabin alongside the trail and, as we descended the sloping trail to the river, we found remnants of a stone building and a stone oven of some sort. Piles of rock sat atop the ledges that rose above the riverbank and were overgrown with grass, weeds, and bushes.

This six-foot-high falls is composed of a series of graded inclines over which the cascades slide, rather than fall. I could picture a group of happy children, yelling as they went down these slick slopes. The fracture lines of the rock over which the water poured, were reminiscent of those we had seen in slate rock formations. Above the falls were several smaller cascades and below the falls was a deep, quiet pool, from which the water meandered downstream. From the bank where we stood, a large birch extended its branches out over the face of the falls in a protective gesture.

Five or six miles northeast of Nonesuch Falls is Greenwood Falls, sometimes called Bonanza Falls, on the Big Iron River. During spring, the water flow is high and spectacular, but it hides one of the falls' most fascinating features—the rock over which it flows. By late summer, low waters reveal the greenish-gray rock fractured in large slabs, leaving sheets of plate-like outcroppings. Much of the rock has a smooth finish similar to hand-rubbed pewter. The river is about 60 feet across and the falls' ledge spans the distance. During low water, visitors can walk most of the way across the river on the rock. At those times, the falls consists of one large cataract on the far side of the river which bounces off submerged split facets of rock as it falls. On the exposed face of the falls, wildflowers grow in the bits of soil trapped in the rock's fracture lines. Part of the rock is sloped into a perfect sun-bathing spot, receiving just enough spray to be refreshing.

Southeast of Greenwood and the many falls of the Porcupine Mountains Wilderness State Park, is Bond Falls, Ontonagon County's best-known falls. This spectacular site, owned since 1947 by the Upper Peninsula Power Company, belonged to Oliver S. Bond of Cleveland, Ohio in 1880. Bond sold the pine timber to a mill which hauled out lumber until 1903. It was then purchased by another logging company in 1916 which cut trees around and up to the falls and river. Several years after fires claimed any surviving growth, young aspens and maples sprang up. A local electric company bought the property in 1931 and by about 1937 built the dam which created the 2,200-acre Bond Lake.

During our visit the trail leading to the falls was along a cement walk which originated at the edge of a parking area. Six cascades, two of which were falls of three to five feet, preceded the main falls. The first of these was no more than 500 feet from the road. A low, unobtrusive retaining wall lined both banks of the river and concrete steps led to the bottom of the major falls. Beside these steps, I found the delicate orange and yellow blossoms of butter-and-eggs growing near the water's edge. After crossing the first of two wooden footbridges, we found ourselves in a lightly forested area where we could view all the facets of this expansive falls. Bond Falls consists of a series of step-like cascades pouring over flat-topped rocks that span the river. The flow over this nearly 60-foot falls was strong and water spurted off the flat rocks in broad, horizontal bands. The foot falls is divided by a rocky outcropping, topped by several trees ringed by a daisy field. A second, wooden footbridge leads to the far riverbank, from where it is possible to walk onto the rocks and stand next to the falls.

Following the Middle Branch of the Ontonagon River downstream five or six miles from Bond Falls will lead the visitor to Agate Falls; larger, but less visited than Bond. The well-marked trail to Agate Falls began at a roadside park and wound down to the riverbed along an incline which was steep in some areas. The path led us onto a large sandy shelf which extended well into the river and allowed us to stand directly in front of the falls. This nearly 80-foot-high falls consists of multiple, powerful cascades billowing out over many ledges of Lake Superior sandstone. The falls spanned the wide river and was uninterrupted by vegetation or exposed rock, even during our late summer visit. The water of the falls seemed to be all white foam, but the large pool at its base was exceptionally clear. The forest grows right up to the falls' escarpment on both sides, but below the pool the riverbanks are lined in summer with wildflowers. Beyond these are stands of young trees, while older, larger pines and some birch stand well back from the river's edge.

Spanning this broad falls is a 100-foot-high trestle bridge which is one of the tallest structures along the Soo Line railroad system. Two young anglers were at work when the sun finally dropped far enough to make the light right for photography, so they became part of C.J.'s portrait of Agate Falls. ■

23

In a
Continuum
Of patterns, water, the
Ultimate chameleon, alters
Its form

Above and at right, Saxon Falls

Pine trees at Overlooked Falls

verlooked Falls

A drop
Of time is lost,
But rivers of time carve
Their impressions on the face of
The earth

Manido Falls

Rocks at Manido Falls

Rock patterns at Greenwood Falls

Crafted
By the river,
This sculpture with satin
Surface, was created by ancient
Forces.
Burnished
By the crumbled
Fragments of past ages,
It remains without a modern
Equal

Above and at right, Bond Falls;
Following pages, anglers at Agate Falls

Steep
rocky ledges
&
gentle
cascades

eweenaw County and the northern part of Houghton County are frequently referred to as "Copper Island" because of the copper that has been mined in this part of the country. Tours are available through several old copper mines in the area which make fascinating interludes between jaunts to waterfalls. In this region, we visited several of Michigan's highest falls. Hungarian Falls, in Houghton County, is a secluded 80- to 90-foot cascade, located half a mile southwest of Hubbell. The falls pours into a gorge once spanned by three mining company trestles—two built in the 1800s and one in 1925. Nothing remains of these structures but bits of their foundations. Still present, but well above the falls, is Hungarian Dam, first built in the late 1800s and rebuilt in 1925 after the original sandstone structure washed out.

Upstream from the main falls is the nearly ten-foot high Upper Hungarian Falls which lies near the old dam and millpond. Here, Hungarian Creek bubbles as a narrow stream toward the rock ledge where it abruptly broadens to form an approximately 15-foot-wide, bridal veil falls crowned with white birch. Part of the water free-falls to the pool, without a ripple of rocky interference.

To find the main section of the falls, we followed a birch-lined path that narrowly skirts the chasm's edge. We visited here both in early spring and again in late summer, and each season presented dramatically different moods. In the spring, the thundering power of the water's flow made everything seem larger, less stable, and a bit more threatening. But by late summer, the scene was changed by warm sunshine, wildflowers, and plush green moss that softened, what was by then, a gently falling stream.

The main falls is formed as the waters of Hungarian Creek pour in broad sheets over a 30- to 40-foot-wide escarpment of Jacobsville sandstone. After striking one of the sandstone ledges, the water billows out in a fine spray which lands as mist on the rock ledges below. The flow empties into a deep basin, then makes a rapid exit rushing over huge boulders as it pours down another, more graded, fall of 40 to 50 feet. Around the base of the falls is a cool glen where moss and ferns grow in lush profusion.

The reduced summer water levels enabled us to climb out toward the base of the falls on boulders which were strewn about in the stream bed like a giant's marbles. A few of the boulders looked newly fallen, but most were covered with moss and lichens indicating long residence in the stream bed. Wildflowers grew between the boulders where water had roared just months before. The cliff face, over which the water falls, looks as if it has been chiseled with a sculptor's tool. Scattered about in the stream bed lay shattered bits of tree trunks, roots, and parts of limbs—some worn smooth by the water—completing testimony to the awesome force of the spring flow.

Many torrents covered, or made inaccessible, most of the rocks upon which we had climbed in the summer. In the spring, huge balls of foam spin about, and a second cascade, located well to the right of the main falls, is created. It is considerably narrower than the main stream, but about 20 feet higher. The water comes across its ledge as a watery wisp which quickly spreads into trails of white mist tripping down the step-like ledges of the narrow groove it has worn into the side of the gorge. We had not noticed the groove in the summer because the trees so tightly border this cascade that summer foliage obscures any trace of it.

ouglass Houghton Falls, also in Houghton County, is approximately three miles northeast of Hungarian Falls. Both the county and the falls are named after Douglass Houghton, Michigan's first state geologist. The falls is impressive and startling, both in its height, and because the viewer comes upon it so suddenly. The trail we followed cut through a high, grassy field filled with wildflowers and berry bushes and abruptly ended at a ledge where the stream drops almost vertically for 160 to 200 feet into a steep gorge. The bottom of the deep ravine is enclosed by almost perpendicular sandstone walls, and although the view from above was excellent, we imagined the view from below would be spectacular! We had been warned, however, not to try descending into the gorge without ropes because the rock is very unstable.

The falls, which was little more than a gentle trickle in the summer, was transformed in early spring to a prodigious, but narrow, flow that fell almost perpendicularly to the ravine floor. The falls was divided in two at its top by a large, centrally located boulder. After re-forming into a single stream, it dropped in long trailing veils until a second boulder divided it once more. It then fell as two streams into the creek bed far below us.

Douglass Houghton Falls is the site of an old copper mine, although only meager quantities of stamp copper were found here. The first of it was discovered in 1845, the same year Houghton was killed in a storm on Lake Superior. The miners had just enough room in the narrow gorge to build a single row of log cabins which provided housing, workshops, and a barn, but they stayed for only two years. All mining here stopped by late 1847, and a cave at the base of the falls is all that remains of the Douglass Houghton Mine.

Keweenaw County boasts not only a rocky coast dotted with clean, sandy beaches; charming towns; and superb fishing; but an assortment of waterfalls as well. We first saw Eagle River Falls from a bridge on the main route through the town of Eagle River. In the calm waters above the falls, a small island sits between riverbanks lined with birch and pine. These trees grow up to the falls' edge on rocky outcroppings where exposed tree roots grasp tenaciously at their hard, unyielding surfaces. During our spring visit, the falls appeared to be nearly 50 feet high, although its actual height may be closer to 25 feet. The water poured over massive bulges of black rock which momentarily split the flow into small streams. A mass of rock protrudes from the center of the falls, and a cave-like depression at its base provides the only spot where water accumulates. There is also a large, rock-filled pool at the base of the falls, from which water slips through a central channel, narrowed by fallen rock. Looking downstream from the bridge, we could see the river enter Lake Superior. We would have loved to see this falls from river level, but the ravine had nearly perpendicular walls, and we could not find any path down. The power of Eagle River Falls had been used for almost 140 years to produce the electricity needed for manufacture of the famous Blight blasting fuse. The Lake Superior Fuse Company, which manufactured these fuses, opened in 1862 and functioned without interruption, until it was destroyed by fire in 1957.

Not far from Eagle River is Jacob's Falls, located on Jacob's Creek. These waters once filled the sluices of the Copper Falls Mining Company, the third largest producer of Keweenaw mass copper. Part of Jacob's Falls is visible from the road as it runs its course through a thick growth of maple trees. At one time, the falls was almost obscured by the trees, but in the early 1970s, trappers removed beaver from the stream, and the unattended beaver dams at the head of the creek began to collapse in domino fashion after a particularly heavy rain. A wall of water roared down Jacob's Creek and destroyed many of the trees as well as a small motel on the highway.

Jacob's Falls pours a sheet of water about 33 feet wide over a series of cascades and rapids. Climbing a steep path along the creek will yield the visitor a good view of the upper cascades, and of the many nearby maple trees that have been bent and twisted by the force of the flowing water. Moss covers much of the rock walls rising above the creek bed and many of the trees as well, infusing everything with an emerald hue. The cascades tumble through a narrow, rocky cleft, some parts of which are a mere four to five feet across. The bottom-most cascade broadens to about fifteen feet after which the waters of Jacob's Creek run jubilantly under the highway and into Lake Superior.

About eight miles west of Jacob's Falls is the Silver River Falls and Cascades. It is actually a small falls which feeds an extensive series of rapids. The falls are located almost directly beneath the bridge over the Silver River, and a one-quarter-mile path follows the river downstream past the rapids and cascades. A small island in the middle of the river downstream is a good place from which to see most of the falling water. It is also an excellent spot to fish for the abundant brook trout. Just below the downstream side of the island, the water slows and quietly slides through the riverbed until it pours into Lake Superior.

From Silver River Falls, we traveled to Copper Harbor, close to the tip of the Keweenaw Peninsula. We were hunting for Manganese Falls—listed in some directories as Manganese Gorge Falls. A local Copper Harbor map showed the

39

falls to be formed by the waters of an unnamed creek flowing from Manganese Lake into Lake Fanny Hooe. The access to the falls is on the road to Estivant Pines, one of the few virgin stands of pine left in Michigan and the home of the 500-year-old "Leaning Giant," second largest white pine in the contiguous 48 states. Though not visible from the car, we found the falls only 200 feet off the road. The sign that had once indicated its presence had been taken down for the winter. Nearly all such signs in this region are taken down in late fall and are not replaced until Memorial Day because they would not survive exposure to Keweenaw County's 200- to 250-inch average snowfall.

The short path to this secluded falls leads to an overlook from which the 50-foot falls can be seen. We were warned not to lean on the aging wooden fence posts that surrounded the overlook and not to stand at the chasm's edge, as there are many unstable overhangs. The gorge walls drop vertically beneath the ledges, creating such a rugged scene that one warning was enough to keep us well back from the fence. The ledges bear tall trees whose branches keep the gorge in shadow, and although we shifted positions and craned our necks, we saw no way to reach the creek bed. The massive gorge is deep and narrow, and the sheer walls are covered with moss.

The noisy, exuberant stream catapulted first in one direction, then another, plunging down the narrow crevasse it had worn in the rock. Not more than six feet across in some places, white water thundered down the narrow slot in six steep tiers making its way to a small pool. At no other falls did we see so much water power concentrated into so narrow a stream. At the end of a dry summer, however, this roaring stream often diminishes to a mere trickle.

Haven Falls, near the village of Lac La Belle, is separated from Manganese Falls by only nine miles as the crow flies, but the moods these two falls create are worlds apart. Haven Falls is located on the edge of a small county park in a quiet woodland setting. A delicate 10-foot cascade is easily visible from the car, but after a bit of climbing, I found that the thin, veil-like flow has three smaller cascades above, and at an angle to it, making the overall height of the falls about 20 feet. After falling over the lowest ledge, the stream crosses two broad rock shelves, cuts through a tree-shaded picnic area, and is crossed by a log footbridge.

Haven Creek and Falls once furnished water power for the Delaware Copper Mill. It was there that the rock, brought from the mine, was crushed to prepare metal concentrates which were then sent to the smelters for refining. One might guess that the name of the stream was derived either from the serenity of this spot or from the refuge sought in the nearby lake by ships encountering foul weather. In truth, it was named for the late Dr. Roscoe R. "Doc" Haven who was head of the local division of the Michigan Highway Department. He was particularly fond of this site and requested that one day it might bear his name. This small falls wears its title well. ■

per Hungarian Falls

Truth is
As elusive
As falling water which
Slips through the grasping fingers of
Dreamers

Middle Hungarian Falls

ung girl at Middle Hungarian Falls   43

Eagle River Falls

Tell me
Where you've been and
Where you've yet to go, but
Soothe me as you pass—for I can't
Follow

Silver River Falls, Keweenaw County

Haven Falls; Following pages, Lake Fanny Hooe

I know
Of a place where
Silence is the language
And time is passed in the nurturing
Of dreams

Deep
rugged canyons
&
rushing
rapids

KEWEENAW BAY AREA

SOUTHERN HOUGHTON & BARAGA COUNTIES

n southeastern Houghton County, about nine and one-half miles north of Sidnaw, lies the Sturgeon River Gorge—sometimes called the Grand Canyon of Michigan. Its 260-foot depth makes it one of the deepest gorges east of the Rockies. As the Sturgeon River flows through this gorge, it forms a powerful 40-foot falls. We made two summer visits to Gorge Falls, one in early June and one in early August, and we began each of them by camping at the U.S. Forest Service Sturgeon River Campground, six miles south of the falls. A number of the campsites are located right on the shores of the river which, at this location, is shallow but swift, clear, and cold. Sitting on the rocks watching the moon reflect like sparklers in the river created an image I will long remember.

Beyond the campground, on the road leading to the falls, is a small semicircular turnout with the remains of an old flume. At the turn of the century, logs were run down the side of the gorge to the river at this spot and then floated downstream. The approximately mile-long trail to the falls is in good condition, and may be easily traveled, although it becomes quite steep in some places. A variety of trees abound along the trail. Sugar maple, is abundant; as is yellow birch, a valuable plywood species; and quaking and big tooth aspen. We also found ironwood, basswood, red maple, black ash, white birch, and black cherry along with at least eight varieties of conifers. The forest floor held more delights; true (or smooth) and false Solomon's seals with their clusters of berries, violets, asters, lily-of-the-valley, wintergreen, bunchberries, thimbleberries, blueberries, club mosses, and ostrich fern. As we approached the river, we faced a formidable red sandstone wall, with numerous overhanging ledges and rock outcroppings, rising 80 to 90 feet from the gorge floor. Proceeding upstream, we discovered bluebead lillies with their brilliant blue, but inedible, berries; and the lovely, purple fringed Habenaria orchid.

Near the falls, a layer of black rock is evident beneath the red Jacobsville sandstone. This rare, geological curiosity represents a portion of the South Range Trap, an ancient lava flow which was uplifted before the sandstone was deposited over it. Over millions of years, the river has gradually eroded this sandstone layer and exposed the lava rock underneath. Huge slabs of this black rock lie scattered on one side of the riverbed, glistening with the mist produced by the thundering waterfall. Ripples in the surfaces of many of the black boulders indicate that this region was once part of an ancient sea. It gives you a strange feeling to realize that today, within a few feet of the falls, there is a very small but fine, sandy beach which is perfect for picnicking.

Sturgeon River Gorge Falls is about 40 feet high and spans the width of the river, which is comparatively narrow in this area. The water plunges over its black ledge with tremendous force, even during summer months, producing large white water-plumes and a heavy shroud of spray. From an overhanging ledge, about 50 feet high, we watched youngsters courageously jump into the deep, frosty-cold pool at the base of the falls.

On the opposite side of the falls, there are no trails, and the forest grows out onto the moss-carpeted ledges which overhang the river. Below the falls, the river broadens as it proceeds downstream toward the sandstone walls. Heading upstream, we climbed the steep, well-worn path the swimmers use to reach their jumping ledge. It brought us above the falls where we discovered a series of rapids and cascades glinting in the sun like gem facets. The top of the gorge is accessible by a trail leading downstream, away from the falls. We watched the river drop away as we followed the trail, continuing to marvel at the unending variation of shapes and forms sculpted in the red sandstone. Several birds had made their homes in the nooks and crannies of the gorge wall, and far below us, on the river's edge, a group of otters played a game of chase-and-slide. The trail eventually turned away from the rim and connected to the path leading back to the road. We found the car and headed west.

When we reached Baraga County, we were once again confronted with a county map that indicated an abundance of waterfalls about which we had little or no information. Frequently, our decision to visit a falls was made rather arbitrarily and depended on such factors as whether the map seemed to indicate fairly good access, whether we liked the name of a falls, whether someone along the road had intriguing stories or information about a particular site, or whether a falls happened to lie in a direction we felt like traveling at that moment. We often wondered if we had unknowingly missed something spectacular.

Of Baraga County's 22 named falls, we visited nine, plus two unnamed cascades. Tibbets Falls is located just three miles north of Watton on the Sturgeon River, but when our attempts to find an access road failed, we stopped at a house to ask directions. On this particular gloomy day that was dampened by a persistent rain, the directions were accompanied by several cups of hot coffee and a personally guided tour to the correct road. Such were the kindnesses of many people we met along the way.

Tibbets Falls is a series of step-like cascades—none of which is greater than four feet in height—with a very gradual, lateral drop of about 20 feet. The cascades run the width of the river tumbling over rock that appears burnished to a fine satin finish. In spite of the rain, we lingered to enjoy the seclusion and to watch the mist rise in opaque streamers from among the trees.

The Sturgeon River Canyon Falls are easily accessible, and facilities have been thoughtfully developed to accommodate picnicking and recreation. The parking area bordering US 41, just south of Alberta, is adjacent to a roadside rest area with picnic tables and restrooms. The one-mile trail to the falls is well-marked, well-maintained, and easily traveled. It takes 15 to 20 minutes to reach the falls, and wooden footbridges carry the visitor over the creek and wet areas.

Near the canyon's rim, the trail is covered with wood-chips and is bordered by wooden railings. Trees along the route are marked with identification plaques, and the species are as varied as those at Sturgeon River Gorge.

In the early 1950s, this falls was almost inaccessible. At that time, it was named Bacco Falls after a contractor who had helped build many of the roads in the area. The falls area was given to Michigan Technological University in 1954 by the Ford Motor Company Fund as part of the Ford Forestry Center. In 1963, Erick Bourdo, director of the Center, initiated the name change. The park area and trail were built with the help of students from the Center, the Youth Conservation Corps of the Michigan Department of Natural Resources, and inmates from the Baraga Conservation Correction Camp. The trail, however, was built only on the north side of the river—the south side has remained untouched.

he falls plunges 20 feet over its ledge into the largest box canyon in Michigan. Approximately 78,000 gallons of water per minute pour into the river below, racing on through a long, narrow, granite canyon with walls rising 30 to 60 feet above the river. The angle of the waterfall's flow to the trail is such that only part of the falls can be seen, and we were unable to reach any area which would afford a better perspective. Adorning the canyon walls are mosses which flourish in the constant mist of the falls. In summer, polypody ferns and wildflowers display themselves on the ledges of the canyon wall and shyly peek from beneath its numerous overhangs. Much of the rock in the area looks like slate but is actually a fine-grained quartzite. Large slabs of rock show the ripple marks that indicate its formation from sand that once lay beneath an ancient sea. Less than one mile east of the Sturgeon River Canyon Falls are granite outcroppings which are believed to mark the southernmost extension of the Canadian Shield, that layer of Precambrian rock which is the bedrock of the North American continent. Bordering the granite is a deposit of graphite which was commercially mined just a few miles north of the falls. The animals and birds in the area must sense that the people who walk these paths mean them no harm, for they were very bold. Birds, chipmunks, squirrels, rabbits, and even frogs seemed at ease with our presence and were intent on keeping us entertained.

Not far from Sturgeon River Canyon Falls is the source of the Falls River. During its ten-mile jaunt to Keweenaw Bay, the river falls nearly 1000 feet in a continuing series of cascades and rapids. It is particularly well-known to anglers for its steelhead runs, but it also boasts sizable populations of brook, brown, and rainbow trout; coho and pink salmon; chinook; smallmouth bass; and smelt—making Falls River understandably popular with local anglers. Of the numerous cascades on the river, we visited two located within the L'Anse city limits and a third on the edge of town. The latter falls, however, was the only one

Sturgeon River Gorge Falls

of the three indicated on the county maps. To differentiate it from the other two, I call it the Upper Falls. It is located just across the road from a new housing development, although, during our visit, none of the impinging "civilization" could be seen from the falls. From the road, the only indication of the falls existence was a well-worn path leading through the trees.

The falls has a sheer drop of eight to ten feet over a ledge that spans the river. The August water flow was confined to one area of the ledge, although the spring waters may cover it completely. Mosses and ferns were growing along the fracture lines of the exposed slate outcroppings, giving the ledge the appearance of a terraced rock garden.

The area is a popular swimming hole, and we watched children dive into the deep pool at the base of the falls. Several bathers swam beneath the falls and stood on a ledge to peer out through the falling water. After C.J. photographed the falls, we sat back to relax and enjoy this delightful spot which seemed so perfectly designed for both swimming and relaxing.

The path that leads to the Middle and Lower Falls on the Falls River begins alongside an industrial plant on the waterfront in L'Anse. There, the Falls River empties into L'Anse Bay, a small section of the larger Keweenaw Bay. Although the path's beginning did not hold the promise that sites of great beauty lay just ahead, we have learned that there is no way to accurately anticipate the nature of a waterfall.

Along the very short walk to the Lower Falls, we encountered dogwood trees, wild raspberries, honeysuckle, chokeberries, and thorn apples. When we reached the falls, we watched its waters slide over gradually inclined slate ledges in gentle cascades. The largest drop was less than five feet. By following the path upstream a short distance beyond the Lower Falls, we reached what I call the Middle Falls. It lies just downstream from a trestle bridge. We passed several stands of handsome white cedar, then clamored down the riverbank, past large clumps of Equisetum, or Scouring rushes, to the wide, multi-ledged falls. The late summer water flow was sparse so the falls consisted of a multitude of tiny rivulets stepping over moss-terraced ledges. We climbed out on the ledges, for the real beauty of this falls lies in the delicate grace of each mini-cascade, and these are more easily appreciated close at hand.

Another small falls which lay just off US 41, south of L'Anse, was Dault's Falls on Dault's Creek. Home for brook and brown trout, Dault's Creek is bordered by cultivated land on one side and forest on the other. During our visit in early May, the stream bed was overflowing its banks—the result of melting winter snows—and the creek appeared to be one long series of rapids and cascades. The actual falls was only five to six feet high and spanned the 25-foot width of the creek. The water flowed smoothly over the first ledge of the falls but exploded into white froth as it hit a second ledge. As far as we could see along its course, the creek raced onward as white water toward its fusion with the Falls River. During the summer, we imagined one might be greeted with a more tranquil scene. With sunlight easily penetrating the lightly forested surroundings, this falls provided a marvelous setting for an afternoon of spring picnicking and fishing.

Skanee Road which heads northeast from L'Anse toward Skanee, is the main route to six of the falls we visited in Baraga County. Of these falls, L'Anse is closest to Silver Falls on the Silver River. Quite different from the Silver River in Keweenaw County, this stream originates at Clear Lake, southeast of Herman, and flows north until it empties at the head of Huron Bay. About one-half mile south of Skanee Road, the river rushes through a narrow gorge in a series of cascades interrupted now and then by areas of calm flow. The riverbed is surrounded by a combination of firs, pines, and maples. It slopes gently downward over a long distance before making a right-angle turn and tumbling ten feet over a slate ledge to form Silver Falls.

our miles east of the Silver River is the Slate River, where we located the scenic Slate River Falls, as well as two other delightful and unnamed falls. The Slate River originates in the Huron Mountains of eastern Baraga County. This river of crystal mountain water forms numerous cascades and large areas of white water on its trip to Huron Bay. It is for these characteristics that it was once known as the Dashing River. In 1872, the discovery of slate on the banks of the river brought about the change to its present name. At that time, slate was needed for roofing, blackboards, and student's slates and within one year, the town of Arvon grew up around a new slate quarry which lay just three miles south of the falls. Employing primarily Irish and Welsh workers, the quarry produced some of the best slate in the world, according to a 1874 article in the *Marquette Mining Journal*. Slate was excavated at Arvon for 13 years, although it never became profitable, and in 1893 the quarry closed. Henry Ford made a brief attempt to reopen it during the 1930s, but today, only a few foundations remain at the site of what was once the town of Arvon.

Slate River Falls is only one-half mile east of Skanee Road, but after having no success in finding it, we stopped at a tavern to get directions. We were guided onto a short dirt road nearby that would take us to the river, and were told to follow the river upstream for about half-a-mile. When we finally found the pathway, we were able to walk at the base of the steep banks bordering the river. Bits of broken rainbow slate in beautiful hues of orange, rose, lavender, periwinkle blue, and yellow lay strewn about the river banks, making the path a visual delight, but also making the trek a bit rough. Slanted sheets of slate rose out of the river's sand like beds of flowers, flaunting intricate fracture patterns in place of blossoms.

Slate River Falls was geologically formed by the upward folding of the slate itself. This produced a slick, fractured slate wall over which the river plunges nearly 25 feet in two streams into a very deep, quiet pool. Reflecting upward from the bottom of the pool through its lucent water were multiple hues of the rainbow slate.

The huge slabs of smooth, black slate that form the backdrop to this falls were bare of plant life, while the walls around the pool bore pine and maples at their top and were draped with the ever-present mosses. We found lichen only on the wall of the pool which was bordered by a slate beach. Lying next to the beach, which we reached by stone-stepping our way across the river, were the 30- to 40-foot horizontal remains of a tree which once must have towered over the falls. The beach is a perfect setting for a picnic, and the pool is a wader's paradise. In addition to the abstract patterns in the slate at our feet, this secluded site was supplied with numerous mushrooms, toads, and frogs. It isn't difficult to reach Slate River Falls, but its access is rather obscure, and the falls are not visible even from the tops of nearby ridges. Seemingly remote from civilization, we nonetheless felt secure surrounded by so much natural beauty. We left Slate River Falls with great reluctance.

Upstream, where the river flows closest to Arvon Road, we encountered two unnamed falls in close proximity to one another. We took the liberty of naming the upper falls, Black Slate Falls, and the lower one, Quartzite Falls. We first saw these two falls in early August. During this very dry season, their black slate ledges were largly exposed except for widely scattered cascades which they seemed to wear almost out of modesty. At Black Slate Falls multiple cascades poured into a quiet, shallow pool bordered by loose slate on one side and a low, vertical, fractured slate wall on the other. This quiet falls, surrounded by a dense growth of white cedar, maples, and pines, had the soft-spoken quality of a fine chamber music orchestra. The falls had a drop of five to seven feet and was 40 to 50 feet across at its broadest point. In April the high water filled the riverbed and obscured all the rock, and with all semblance of tranquility gone, the river raced to a much faster tune.

On the road between Black Slate and Quartzite Falls are the remains of the famous Iron Range and Huron Bay Railroad which was built in the late 1800s in an attempt to transport iron from the area. The project was abandoned during its test run, however, when the locomotive faltered at the base of a steep incline and derailed. On the river, near this site, an attempt was also made to float logs downstream using wing dams, but it was also unsuccessful. When it failed, another railroad—this one successful—was built to haul lumber.

Just below a footbridge upstream from Quartzite Falls, the Slate River becomes shallow. In the summer months, when the water levels are lowest, perfectly straight ridges of white quartzite could be seen running through the riverbed in varying widths, and criss-crossing at angles. In late April, however, the heavy water flow obscured these fascinating formations.

In usually drier summer months, the water falls over three ledges in gentle cascades and slips down a rocky incline that makes a great water slide that is especially popular with local swimmers. In spring, however, the falls tumbles over three tiers and the slide actually becomes a rushing current of white water. The entire drop, including the slide, is about 15 feet.

During this high water period, the slate fracture lines were only evident on ledges surrounding the top of the falls. There are numerous rocky shelves on the riverbank, where we sat and dangled our feet in the water as the cool weather made swimming prohibitive. Growing on these fractured ledges were lichens, mosses, and small ferns arranged in intricate patterns. There is a special feeling of discovery after encountering an unmapped falls such as this one. It was as if we were suddenly privileged to share some treasured secret.

Another of Baraga County's well-kept secrets is Erik's Falls. Even though it is marked on the maps, and thus is less private than Quartzite Falls, this falls is still comparatively obscure because of its more remote location. One of several falls located on the West Branch of the Huron River, this small falls is among the most pleasant and secluded sites we found. Beneath a small bridge, a series of tumbling cascades bubble into a crystal-clear pool which is perfect in summer for a waist-high splash. From the pool, the water pours over a rocky rim to the river about five feet below. The rim is worn jeweler's-wheel smooth and has holes and indentations arranged in cubistic patterns. The rim spans the river's 35-foot-width and was exposed during the summer months, but its wear patterns suggest it is completely covered by the spring flow. During our summer visit, the water forming the main falls flowed quickly downstream into the rocky riverbed where it formed three, smaller, gentler cascades. Within arm's length of the falls is an ideal campsite with room for a tent, plenty of fallen timber for firewood, a fresh spring nearby, and an absence of mosquitos.

Four miles north of Erik's Falls and just downstream from Big Eric's Bridge, where the East and West Branches of the Huron River join, is Big Eric's Falls. The bridge was named for one of the earliest loggers in the area who built the bridge so he could haul his lumber to L'Anse. The falls is composed of two separate two-foot cascades. After passing over the first cascade, the river bends around a ledge and continues over the second cascade. Much of the rock in the riverbed was exposed during our summer visit revealing areas where the river has undercut its rocky banks at the bend.

The meadow-like area around the falls was, in summer, surrounded by small trees and wildflowers. The smell of freshly cut grass was strong and sweet. This is a fine recreation area complete with picnic tables, reports of good fishing, and a nearby state forest campground. ■

Detail of Upper Falls on Falls River

I sought
To capture the
Fall's power in my hand
And found I had caught nothing but
A tear

Upper Falls on Falls River

ddle Falls on Falls River

Lower Falls on Falls River

er Falls, Baraga County

So small
Amidst giants!
Is it a miracle
That I alone stand as the sun's
Focus?

Above and at right, birch trees at Sturgeon River Gorge Falls

Slate River Falls

Slate formations at Slate River Falls

Slate River Falls

With a
Calm persistence,
The marsh consumes its foes
Marking each grave with fragile white
Lilies

Marsh near Sturgeon River Gorge Falls

Spring runoff, Black Slate Falls

When you
Are embraced but
Not encumbered, and when
You're held but not imprisoned, you
Are loved

Rock patterns at Erik's falls; At right, Erik's Falls;
Following pages, Black Slate Falls

Ever-changing
patterns
&
sparkling
reflections

NORTH CENTRAL UPPER PENINSULA

MARQUETTE AND ALGER COUNTIES

 he waterfalls we visited in Marquette and Alger Counties, with the exception of the Black River Falls, are all within ten miles of Lake Superior's southern shore. Black River Falls, not to be confused with the group of falls by the same name in Gogebic County, is the most westerly of the four falls we saw in Marquette County. From the parking lot at the Black River Campgrounds, we followed a short, well-marked path to a bridge that spans a section of the river separating a small island from the river bank. The bridge afforded an excellent view of this powerful falls but curiosity prevailed, so we climbed down off the cement blocks at the end of the bridge and out onto the rocks of the island. From there, we had an even more spectacular view for we directly faced the falls.

The river came into view from the left, turned almost 90 degrees, and then roared through a narrow, rock-filled gorge. Like violent fountains, great plumes of water erupted from behind those rocks throwing a constant stream of bubbles and spray into the air. After falling 25 to 30 feet, the water spilled into a large, quiet pool filled with suds. The river then split to flow around the island, fused to a single channel beyond it, and continued on its way.

Our island observation post was covered with blueberries which were the highlight of our afternoon snack. The constant spray from the falls brought cool respite from the August heat, while the pool around us mirrored the slow passage of large, white clouds. Dark, almost purple, lichen clung to a rock wall beside us.

We returned to Black River Falls the following year in early May. Gone was all tranquility of our previous visit! The island was almost totally submerged, and the water's thunder was so great that we had to yell to hear one another. Even while standing on the bridge, the spray from the falls reached the camera's lens, and the riverbed was filled with white water as far downstream as we could see. Black River was still beautiful, but its veneer of gentle summer innocence had been stripped away to reveal the water's raw power.

Alder Falls is located northwest of Marquette, one mile south of Lake Independence, and about two miles southeast of Big Bay. This charming falls is definitely off the beaten track. The trail to Alder Falls is bordered with abundant tall birch, so white they almost seem lit from within. During our visit, their luminescent glow provided sharp contrast to the misty gloom of intermittent rain which had timed its arrival to ours. As we followed a curving trail, we heard the throaty hum of the falls well before we caught sight of it. The trail descended somewhat steeply to reveal a swiftly flowing creek which poured over a slight grade. The river made a sharp turn away from us and charged over a precipice which swung it back toward where we stood. The billowing plumes falling over the five-foot-high ledge quickly broadened out into white sheets of foam as the falls spread over a gradually inclined rock face. Looking much like a bride's train, the water dropped about 15 to 18 feet in multiple steps. After its main descent, the water continued to drop another 15 to 20 feet down a very gradual grade before the stream bed leveled out. Large boulders lay strewn in the water's path as if to convince doubters of the intense power of the water's flow.

Along the creek, many pines were intermingled with the majestic birch. Both were growing up to the waters' edge and towered far above the falls. During our visit, the moisture in the air combined with the spray from the falls to envelop the trees in mist, creating images with the quality of a faded photograph. All sound was drowned out by the tumultuous pounding of the water. At Alder Falls, we were more acutely aware of the water's potential force than at many of the larger, more impressive falls.

ecause it was not marked on our maps, we encountered Warner Falls quite by accident. Located on Warner Creek, south of Negaunee, we first saw this falls from the road, and climbed down the steep embankment to get a better look. This 20-foot-high falls was flowing with the enthusiasm that only a spring melt can bring. The water poured over a narrow crest to a broad base and into a shallow pool. After a brief respite, it slid down a gradual incline and formed a small set of rapids. The side of this falls nearest the road is treeless, but there are beautiful white birch on the opposite bank. The area, however, has been spoiled by the presence of old tires and assorted trash. There was also a strong odor which we attributed to the refuse but which may actually be caused by the natural leaching of minerals coming out of the rock deposits into the water itself. Warner Falls is a potentially lovely site, worth noting by passing travelers.

The last falls in Marquette County that we sought was Upper Chocolay Falls, indicated on our maps as being located on the East Branch of the Chocolay River. Nearby, but on the West Branch of the Chocolay River, was Frohling Falls whose location on the map indicated it might be difficult to reach so we decided to bypass it. After having no luck finding Upper Chocolay Falls, we asked directions locally and were told that the names and locations of both falls are confused on the county maps. We were then given directions to what our guide called Upper Chocolay Falls (Frohling Falls on our map) with the admonition that we would cross private property and should first obtain permission from the residents.

The following day, we obtained both permission and a guided tour from a resident at the farmhouse on the property. I noticed that she, too, called the falls Upper Chocolay Falls as she led us through a pasture and one-quarter mile downstream to their location.

The falls was approximately 30 to 40 feet across at its base and was oddly wedge-shaped. We estimated the far side of the falls to be about 11 feet high and the near side only five feet high. Rocky ledges, rising above the top of the falls, guarded both its sides. These ledges were covered to their rims by ferns and trees heavy with moss. The water catapulted between these tree-topped stony restraints with great power and force. Crossing its precipice smoothly, the water quickly encountered the first of several ledges off which it bounded, throwing fingers of foam into the air. Further impacts on several more ledges, produced white plumes. The water then thundered across a large, horizontal rock face. This was a beautiful spot, lush with ferns and mosses which appeared to coat everything, giving the area a softened, almost carpeted appearance.

Leaving Marquette County and moving east, we entered Alger County. This county is probably best known for the Pictured Rocks National Lakeshore, but it also has many beautiful and unusual waterfalls. Laughing Whitefish Falls, in the northwest quadrant of the county, just north of Sundell, qualifies on both accounts because of the obliquely inclined and multi-fractured rock face over which the falls spill. The walk to Laughing Whitefish is pleasant and easy, leading directly to the head of the falls. From that point, a steep set of wooden steps descends into the gorge which would otherwise be inaccessible to non-climbers such as ourselves. At the base of the steps, we noticed a large, cave-like depression in the cliff wall with remnants of old campfires at its mouth. A steep path continued from the base of the steps to the base of the falls.

At the top of the falls, the waters of Laughing Whitefish River fall vertically over two ledges. The flow then encounters a huge, gently sloping, wedge-shaped rock face whose surface is fractured into countless tiny ledges. During our visit, foamy-white sheets of water slid over the mini-steps across half of the wedge. The water falls a total of 90 to 100 feet into a gorge whose walls rise high above it, creating an amphitheater-like setting. The enigma here is that the star performer never leaves center stage, but is continually making an exit.

April's rains had spilled into the first week of May and had been following us for several days. This day was no exception! It was raining much too hard to climb the stairs and reach the car without getting soaked, so we ducked into the cave. We were not the only ones with that idea for we found another couple already there. During the next half hour, the four of us listened to the staccato sound of hail on rock and watched the icy spheres ricochet into the cave. When the rain slowed to a drizzle we headed out, leaving behind the unusual ledge-stepping beauty of Laughing Whitefish Falls.

About five miles northeast of Laughing Whitefish Falls is Rock River Falls, one of the most remote in the county. This secluded falls is formed by the Rock River which, over thousands of years, has carved a canyon that averages 200 feet in depth and a quarter of a mile in width. We have been told that the canyon is truly impressive in the winter when the gorge walls are not shrouded by vegetation and when numerous ice caves are present.

We traveled to Rock River Falls in a four-wheel drive vehicle late one June day, naive of the terrain, but confident we were well prepared. In the process, we suffered innumerable black fly and mosquito bites, spent half a day trying to locate roads which did not exist, got a four-wheel drive vehicle stuck, and finally had to be led to the falls by a local youngster. Our guide took us into a small glen and out onto a rocky beach which faced the falls. From that vantage point, we watched the Rock River fall 12 to 15 feet over a broad ledge to form a perfect bridal veil. To the right and left of the falls, a rock wall curved toward us forming a semicircular arena. Ferns draped the ledges, and mosses turned rock to velvet. The falling water poured into a quiet pool that lay between the pebble-strewn beach on which we stood and the falls themselves. Exiting through a narrow channel to our left, the water bubbled its way out of sight.

As delightful as we found Rock River Falls, we did not explore the area around it because the insect onslaught was extraordinary. We protected ourselves as best we could, but it was especially difficult for C.J. who could not wear the mosquito netting while focusing his camera. Whenever he got under the darkcloth, he was accompanied by deerflies, black flies, mosquitoes, and no-see-ums. During our stay in the canyon, each of us acquired a glimmering halo of insects that persisted in following us back to the car in spite of our mosquito netting. We recommend exploring Rock River Canyon before June or after July.

Not far from Rock River, just seven miles south of Au Train, is the more accessible Au Train Falls. This falls is separated from a parking area by a short dirt path which leads onto a low, wooden bridge spanning the river. We arrived in August and found thin, wispy rivulets of water stepping over a plethora of ragged ledges. We were told that the water drops 100 feet from the crest of the falls to its base, but because of the gentle grade, the height is difficult to appreciate. A dam which restricts the water flow is located above the falls. In addition, the water is diverted from the riverbed into culverts that pass through a small powerhouse.

The beauty of this falls is found in its exposed and fragmented rock formations. The steps of the falls are formed by rock shelves produced by the fracture of the rock along broad, smooth planes. The various hues within the rock of the riverbed are beautifully blended in a continuum of changing patterns. As we left, we noticed rivulets of clear water flowing from the rocky wall bordering the trail. Having arisen from an underground spring, the water was icy cold and delicious as it streamed over the multicolored rocks, trailing mosses caught in its flow.

For delicate charm, no falls of those we visited could match Scott Falls, located just a few yards off M-28 between Christmas and Au Train. The falls lies at the bottom of a sloping hill bordering the road. It was more visible from the road in April than when we had visited the previous August, but I have spoken with a number of people who have routinely traveled M-28 in the summer and were unaware of the falls' existence.

Just before reaching Lake Superior, the waters of Scott Creek pour over a rock outcropping that overhangs a small cave or grotto. At the top, a large rock in

Laughing Whitefish Falls

the stream bed briefly divides the flow in half. The water drops 10 to 12 feet into a small, almost still, pool and then continues on to form the proverbial babbling brook. This lovely falls had a kind of classic beauty that brought to mind old movies with similar waterfalls accompanied by Pacific Island bathing beauties wearing flowers in their hair.

I was able to walk behind the falls into the grotto. Once inside, I peered back out into the sunlight through wet ferns and moss hanging from the escarpment into the falls like tangled strands of witch's hair. The cave contains a rare moss, *Schistostega pennata,* which is secreted away in the crevasses of its roof. Commonly known as luminous moss, cave moss, or goblin gold, this species is usually found only in damp, dark places such as caves associated with sandstone, under old barns, or in cavities under the roots of upturned trees. Other than a few areas near Upper Tahquamenon Falls and in the cave at Scott Falls, I could find no other account of its occurrence in Michigan. When sunlight entered the cave at a low angle, such as it did at sunset, the moss reflected the light like tiny chips of golden-green emeralds.

In strong contrast to the sun-splashed tranquility of Scott Falls, was the moodiness of Wagner Falls south of Munising. The parking area for the falls is immediately adjacent to the highway, but the sound of the falls could be heard over the highway noises even at roadside. A plaque on a rock at the beginning of the path gives credit to the Michigan Division of the Women's Farm and Garden Association for donating the area to the state of Michigan. After walking through a dense growth of maples, firs, and yellow birch, we crossed a wooden footbridge and saw the first small cataracts. A view of the main falls quickly followed, but the trail continued across Wagner Creek and up to the very edge of the falls.

Wagner is a double-tiered falls with a small upper cascade and 10- to 12-foot lower cascade. Ferns drape themselves along the fringes of the falls and maples protrude over the falls' bottom shelf. A small fir tree was growing in the middle of the stream bed beneath the falls, grasping at the rocks as the river cascaded around it. Standing at the edge of the falls that overcast day produced a mood usually associated with crumbling Victorian mansions seen under foreboding skies. The surrounding dense woods makes the falls area seem remote, despite its close proximity to the highway.

From the base of the falls, the upper cascades are somewhat hidden from view. They are accessible, however, via a steep, slippery slope on the right side of the falls. At the top of the falls, the water drops over a few rocky steps before catapulting over one larger ledge. As I looked down from the top cascades, the trail to the lower falls was not visible, and the feeling of being isolated became more intense. Some of the trees at the upper falls are old and twisted into strange forms. Some actually grow horizontally out of the stream bank before turning in a vertical climb toward the sun. When we left, the twilight was dense with grey mist and heavy with the musty odor of the forest. We walked the path back to the car in pensive silence.

Only one-half mile northeast of Wagner Falls is the fragile Alger Falls whose waters can be seen from the highway. At its top, the flow is divided into two small cascades which tumble over a broad step-like ledge and fall about four feet to a continuing series of ledges below. The water then disappears in the undergrowth and emerges as a small, enthusiastically running brook of multiple, tiny cascades.

The path that led toward the falls was bordered by daisies, buttercups, and tall, pink thistles when we visited. As I climbed past small firs and maples that had gained footholds along the ledges, the sound of the falls overcame highway noises even though the road was still in sight. The path ended before I reached the top, but the crest was accessible by climbing over some slick rock.

At the crest of the falls, the vibrant reds and browns of the rock blended with the greens of the thriving moss to form a beautiful abstract montage. Below, I could see a small pool, not previously visable, into which the water descended before disappearing into the underbrush.

Just northeast of Alger Falls is the western boundary of Pictured Rocks National Lakeshore. Three of the last four falls we visited in Alger County are located within the park's boundries; Munising, Miner's, and Sable Falls. Although Chapel Falls is not part of the national lakeshore, sections of Chapel Lake into which it flows are within park limits.

Munising Falls, the most westerly of the four, is only one-and-one-half miles east of downtown Munising. During our visit, the U.S. Park Service was altering the parking lot and path to the falls. We had walked no more than 50 feet along the trail before we heard the sound of rushing water. Maples and sparkling white birch trees lined the banks of the stream—some nearly 60 feet tall. Small cascades tumbled by us, becoming larger as we neared the falls. Small blueberry patches dotted the side of the trail which led over two small footbridges; the second of which afforded us our first view of Munising Falls. About 70 feet above us, a veil-like flow of water soared over a precipice through a narrow crevice in the rock. It cascaded over a sheer sandstone escarpment which forms the walls of a large, natural amphitheater whose geological formation is the same as that of the Pictured Rocks. Once over its ledge, the catapulting flow threw itself about 50 feet down onto the rock below where it is slowly carving a depression. The jack-hammer sound of the water pounding against the rock was amplified as it echoed off the sandstone walls. So intense was the sound that it made me feel I could see the rock wear away under the water's impact. I was tempted to step under the falls to escape the hot August sun but the force of the water's flow discouraged me. From its impact point on the rock, the water slipped over a smaller, slanted ledge into a large pool and then into the stream bed, forming the small cascades that we had encountered at the beginning of the path.

The path continued from the base of the falls toward the cliff face and then led behind the falls themselves. Looking up from the base of the cliff, I could see lichens and mosses clinging to their precarious footholds. The top of the falls was trimmed with white birch, a few of which grew straight out from the rock face. Poised as quiet guardians, some of the trees growing near the base of the cliff rose as high as the crest itself. The mosses on the rock behind the falls flourished in the spray thrown upward as the water pounded against the rock ledge. The grass at the front edges of the falls was in constant motion, stirred by the air moved about by the water's powerful pounding. Along the right side of the bank, buttercups were glistening with moisture and highlighted by the sun.

Without even getting damp, I walked behind the falls into the natural concavity at the base of the bluff. The sun was shining through the falling water, projecting dancing shadows onto the rock face like the flickering of an old-time movie. Looking outward, I could almost feel the power of the water's flow as it hurtled by me in free flight. It is this power which produced, and will continue to alter, the face of this magnificent falls.

lso within the boundaries of the Pictured Rocks Lakeshore, is Miner's Falls. We reached the falls via a clearly marked dirt road. This same route also leads to Miner's Castle—an imposing rock formation perched on a cliff 100 feet above the waters of Lake Superior. The drive to Miner's Falls was lined with towering birches and maples, as was the mile-long path from the parking area. The trees were so tall that their tops formed an umbrella through which little sunlight was able to filter. The forest floor, therefore, was devoid of plant life except ferns, mosses, and a few young pines trying to find their own place in the sun.

The path to the falls began in a field filled with common mullein. The walk continued through the forest and was easy and pleasant with benches placed along the path. At the point where we first heard the falls, a wooden staircase descended the side of the gorge and ended at a platform situated well above river level from which we had an unobstructed view of the falls. There appeared to be no access to the bottom of the gorge near the falls except by descending to river level at some point downstream and then walking back, so we were content with our vantage point.

The water enters from the right in a series of small cascades that, upon reaching the ledge of the escarpment, free-falls 75 feet in a single, white torrent. As it reaches its base, the water spills behind a boulder before finishing its race to Lake Superior. As we watched, the foam generated by the falls clung to the rocks like masses of white moss. The smooth, steep cliff face was punctuated by deep holes bored into it by the force of the water. Large trees stood at a distance from the water's violent force. The power with which the falls hit the rocks below sent

Birch tree near Black River Falls

up a constant stream of spray. This is a falls to be viewed with awe and respect.

Four miles northeast of Miner's Falls, secluded among imposing hardwoods, lies Chapel Falls. The location of this magnificent falls appeared only on our DNR map. The first time we drove the dirt road leading to Chapel Falls, the weather was dry and there had been logging activity in the area. The logging company was maintaining the road and we found it in excellent shape. When we returned the following May, the road was in poor condition because of a wet spring and the cessation of logging activity, but it was still passable. Many such secondary roads in the Upper Peninsula can be in excellent condition during one season, and in severe disrepair the next. This unpredictability lends greater adventure to any U.P. travel.

The first part of the trail leading to the falls was adorned with assorted wildflowers growing beneath large maples. As we followed the path, the number, size, and variety of hardwood trees increased to include American beech, white and yellow birch, and mountain ash sporting bright red berries.

After walking about half an hour, we heard the vibrating thrum of the falls accompanied by the choraling of birds. Leaving the main trail, we cut through the trees to our left and were rewarded with our first look at the falls. Although it was somewhat obscured by trees which grow on the cliff face below, we found ourselves peering into a deep sandstone gorge with steep, heavily wooded walls. Into this gorge flows Chapel Falls. Beginning as a small stream, the waters of Section Creek crept out to the edge of an escarpment where they broke into three cascades which plummeted over a ledge. Fusing into one larger cascade, the water continued downward, first in multiple tiers over a fan-shaped rock and then in thin swirling sheets spread in changing patterns over an angled rock face. Another series of cascades preceded the water's entry into a small pool. Leaving the pool, the water formed a final set of cascades before disappearing from view in the foliage below. The total vertical drop is about 150 feet.

The amphitheater backdrop for this falls was bare of trees, and lichen grew only on the upper ledges. White birch crowned the top of the falls behind which we rock-hopped our way across the stream. The path continued on the other side, following the edge of the cliff and ended in a small clearing which afforded a spectacular view of the falls. We could see only the tops of the woody giants whose roots were somewhere in the gorge below. Pine trees sweetened the air with their fragrance.

We settled back to enjoy this spot and after lunch I went exploring. I walked across the clearing, away from the falls, and stood on a ledge from which Chapel Lake was visible in the distance. Below this ledge was a 15-foot drop to a well-worn trail leading to the pool and lower portions of the falls. The climb down was tricky, requiring a bit of agility, a touch of insanity, and a lot of care, but the trail beyond it was easy to follow. ■

Movements
Choreographed
By the wind, are danced by
Graceful limbs, in a motionless
Ballet

Birch trees near Alder Falls

lger Falls

Warner Creek Falls

ohling Falls

Countless
Lacy fingers
Flutter with hushed applause,
Hailing the whispered passage of
The wind

Ferns near Rock River Falls

Wagner Falls

Tranquil
Daydreams live in
Moss-lined grottos and swim
In pools fed by streams of molten
Sunlight

Miner's Falls

That which
Is reflected
Is as vulnerable
To the touch of man as is its
Image

eds and Reflections, Alger County

Pine tree graveyard near Chapel Falls

pel Falls; Following pages, Alder Falls, birch trees near Alder Falls

Powerful
and majestic,
the large
and small

SOUTH CENTRAL UPPER PENINSULA & LOWER PENINSULA

DICKINSON, DELTA, LUCE, CHIPPEWA AND PRESQUE ISLE COUNTIES

pper Tahquamenon Falls in Luce County is Michigan's best known and most visited falls. Located in Michigan's second largest state park, it is the second largest waterfall east of the Mississippi, bested only by Niagara. About 8,000 years ago, near the end of the last glacial advance, the retreating glacier uncovered an old Cambrian sandstone cuesta which created Tahquamenon. Four centuries ago, the banks of the Tahquamenon River were home to Ottawa and Chippewa Indians, and more recently, the river was immortalized in Longfellow's poem, "Song of Hiawatha."

The road to Tahquamenon is well-marked with highway signs indicating directions and distances. Visitors can park in a large, paved lot adjacent to the park's gift shop and snack bar, and from there it is only a 3/8-mile walk along a paved path to the gorge area and falls. The path is heavily forested with a variety of trees including sugar maple, white cedar, American beech, white birch and balsam fir, and it branches near the river. The right fork leads to the crest of the falls where there is a large viewing platform. We followed the left fork which was bordered that early June by Canadian mayflowers, starflowers, pink lady's slippers, and mouse-ear chickweed. Descending a long flight of wooden steps into the gorge downstream from the falls, we reached a wooden boardwalk that leads along the river through an area of the gorge which otherwise would be inaccessible to most visitors. There are two observation platforms along the boardwalk; the second and larger of which affords an excellent view of the falls.

The falls drops nearly 50 feet over a single precipice that is more than 200 feet wide. A maximum water flow of greater than 50,000 gallons per second has been recorded at this falls. The golden-brown color of the water, as it billows out over its sandstone escarpment, is said to be caused by the tannic acid released into the water by the decaying vegetation in cedar swamps where the river originates. Falling to the riverbed below in one uninterrupted cascade, the water explodes off large, semi-submerged boulders in clouds of mist before flowing on through the broad riverbed.

The rocky escarpment over which the water falls, extends laterally to both sides beyond the falls, forming an amphitheater-like backdrop. The trees around the river and falls grow right up to the waters' edge, often extending out over the water. This is one of the oldest beech-maple climax forests in the U.S. with trees 300 to 400 years old.

Four miles east of the Upper Falls lies Lower Tahquamenon Falls—officially in Chippewa County, but still within the state park. Here, the woodpeckers were drumming a staccato symphony. The several-hundred-foot walk from the car to an overlook is surrounded by white birch with multiple trunks beneath which, in season, lie dense clusters of lovely white, four-petaled bunchberries. The Lower Falls consist of five separate cascades lying on both sides of a large island in the center of the river. The island can be reached by renting a rowboat at the park concession. A path on the outer rim of the island winds past all five cascades.

Beyond and to the left of the overlook, two of the straw-colored cascades can be seen. The area between the overlook and the cascades is dotted with small, bush-covered islands. Rocky ledges protrude above each of the falls and trees grow to the waters' edge. We viewed this left arm of the river while peering through the intermeshed boughs of a white birch, a red pine, and a white cedar.

A short path leading to the falls on the right arm of the river passes through the trees and over many wooden footbridges. Along the riverbank, swirls of white foam in ever-changing patterns floated by. Two fishermen stood in the swirling waters below the first two-tiered cascade which appeared to have a combined height of about 14 feet. Not far beyond the first falls is a second, smaller cascade. We reached a small, flat, rocky plateau which protruded into the river in front of one of the broadest sections of the cataracts. Above the second falls was a third which was a multiple series of cascades with a main drop of about five feet. The larger cascades wore a constant halo of mist in which rainbows appeared whenever the sun blinked from behind passing clouds. I sat at the edge of the projecting plateau and watched the water race within inches of my feet. Looking at the falls had the same mesmerizing effect as staring into a fire.

The once numerous natural waterfalls of the south-central Upper Peninsula have been reduced in number by the installation of several dams and hydro-electric plants. One undisturbed site in Dickinson County is Fumee Falls, located in a state roadside park along US-2 between Quinnesec and Norway. Fumee is composed of separate upper and lower falls. The vertical height of the lower portion is about 20 feet, falling most of its distance over an obliquely-angled rock face. Between two rocky promontories at the top of the falls, the water has cut a channel five to six feet across and falls the first distance in three short, vertically aligned steps. Below that point, the water spreads over an inclined area of rock debris forming multiple cascades reminscent of the design one might find in an Oriental garden. From its 20-foot-wide base, the waters of the falls run through a grassy flat and into a shallow brook.

I climbed up the steep path on the right side of Fumee Falls past the maples, birches, firs, and pines, and found two more small falls. Fumee Creek pours in from the left, and falls in two streams over a sheer six-foot ledge. From there, the streams entered a small pool partially hidden by trees whose bases were decorated with newly blossomed buttercups. After its momentary respite, the water flow turns 90 degrees and falls another five to six feet. This section of the falls is divided in two by a rocky promontory topped with grass and one tree determined to resist the waters' pull. The water then forms one more small pool before cascading over beautiful moss-covered rocks—flowing on to form the lower falls. This upper pool was marvelous for some toe-splashing though it proved too rocky for wading. I took advantage of this idyllic spot to relax and catch up on daydreaming.

In the 1870s, this was an active mining area. By 1872, the railroad running above the falls had reached Crystal Falls and Iron River, and 22 mines made ore shipments that year. The biggest mines in the area were the Breen and the Vulcan. They shipped out more than 10,000 tons of iron ore in 1877, just after the railroad was built as far as Quinnesec, one-half mile east of the falls.

From there, we headed north toward the little town of Felch, having been told about a falls at Mill Pond produced by the waters of Sundholm Creek. We christened this falls Mill Pond Falls, as it was unnamed on the map. The creek runs out of Mill Pond which is the size of a small lake, its still waters reflecting the rocky ridges, birch, pine, and spruce that surround its shores. We walked downstream along an easily followed footpath until we came to a cascade. The stream bed there was 10 to 12 feet across and in its center was a rocky hillock bearing spruce and birch trees. Between that point and the falls, the water flow was gentle and undisturbed. The path became more difficult and there was a sudden drop in the level of the stream bed, preventing a good look at the face of the falls until we descended to river level.

The rock in the area is fascinating—light in color but heavily stained with red and occasional streaks of green. In addition, the pale green lichen which grows on many of the red areas of the rocks produces a pleasing blend of colors.

This falls' flow was powerful when we contrasted it with the serenity of the pond that fed it. At the top of the falls, the water has cut a channel through dark gray rock and is divided here into two sections by a rocky prominence. The two sections plunge over their escarpment angled toward one another, forming a V-shaped flow of white froth. As we watched, the force of the water hurtling over its ledge produced clouds of fine mist. Not far from the agitated, foam-filled pool at the base of the falls was an accumulation of logs that projected across the stream and considerably slowed the flow of the water. These appeared to be discards from the mill farther upstream and many looked as though they had been part of this "dam" for quite some time. The log jam looked fairly stable and had collected a big glob of foam at its edge.

Our last waterfall stop in the Upper Peninsula was in Delta County, about seven miles northeast of Rapid River. Although our maps showed a U.S. Forest Service campground at Haymeadow Creek, there was no set of "squiggles" on the map to indicate a falls. We had been told, however, that there was a falls at that location and although small, it was a lovely site. We had long since learned that to some people a small falls was anything over one foot high, while to others anything under 20 feet was insignificant. We felt that any falls was worthy of investigation since it was not always the largest that were the most beautiful.

A sign at the campground directed us to "Start Haymeadow Falls Trail." After about 15 minutes of walking it was apparent that we were nowhere near water; and although we were walking through a lovely area of large replanted pines, we decided that somehow we had lost the trail. After all the obscure waterfalls we had hunted down, I couldn't believe we'd get lost at one that had signs. We back-tracked and found that a hundred yards or so from the trail's head, the path turned right...but we had not. Without detours, the walk to the falls passing through a forest of birch, spruce, pine, and maple took about 10 minutes.

A wooden bridge crosses the 20-foot width of Haymeadow Creek just below the falls. During our visit, the creek was swift and shallow but had no rapids. Above the falls, the stream made a Z-shaped turn before reaching the small escarpment over which it fell. On the far side of the falls was a cascade which fell to the stream bed below in a single large plume. The near side of the falls was a large table-top shelf of limestone which overhung the rock beneath. Across its surface ran a few delicate streams which spilled over the ledge.

Although there is no well-defined pool at the base of the falls, a small area is deeper than the rest of the stream. A birch lay across the stream suspended like a bridge. Haymeadow Falls was a pleasant spot, tucked away in the woods and designed for relaxation.

The last in this waterfall collection, and the only waterfall on public property in the Lower Peninsula, is Ocqueoc Falls. Situated in the Black Lake region of Presque Isle County, it is north of M-68 between Onaway and Rogers City. Across the road from the turn to the falls is Ocqueoc River State Forest Campground which has several campsites right on the river. The property across the road, on which the falls is located, was purchased from private owners in 1939 by the state's conservation department. Prior to that time, the Ocqueoc River was controlled by three dams which serviced several thriving lumber mills that began operating in the late 1880s. We found the remains of Luft Dam, one of the three, not far upstream.

After parking, we reached the falls by first passing through a meadow where the sweet smell of buds opening in early April was in the air. To our left, the Ocqueoc River was snaking around a series of bends to form a descending torrent of small cascades. On the other side of the meadow, splendid twin birches stood to the right of the path whose steppingstone rocks led down the sandy riverbank to the waters' edge.

The river's cascades culminated in a six- to eight-foot falls spanning the width of the river. What Ocqueoc Falls lacked in height it made up in pure enthusiasm. The power and thunder of this falls was tremendous. The water pouring over the near side of the falls, which had a sharp drop, appeared as wild, silver hair blowing in the wind. The flow on the far side of the falls spilled over in

Lower Fumee Falls

multiple billows. The cliff face on the far side of the river looked as if it had been constructed of cobblestones.

Farther downstream was another smaller version of the main falls. We reached it by following a footpath that ran alongside the river. As we reached the smaller falls, the path smoothed out and the steep rocky bank on the other side of the river tapered off to water level. Only about two feet high, this lower falls also spanned the river's width and seemed almost as powerful and noisy as its upstream neighbor. On the falls' far side, the water spilled over its ledge and disappeared, only to billow up from behind a rock in a plume of white froth. This site was too tempting for an avid wader, such as myself, to pass up. Meanwhile, C.J. searched along the riverbank for the best spot from which to photograph this lusty falls.

By mid-afternoon, the rapids leading to the falls glistened crystal-white in the sunlight. But as the sun slipped down in the sky, the falls looked straw-yellow in contrast to the brown rock and white froth. At the lower falls, we watched small fish trying to jump up through the cascades. Lulled by the constant hum of the falls, we succumbed to a nap under a nearby tree. When we finally left, the light was fading so perhaps it was an illusion, but I could swear that some of the flower buds that were closed when we arrived, had begun to open.

After two years, four trips, lots of writing, and hundreds of images, we felt we had enough material to do this book. C.J. still agonizes over the many images he felt he left behind, and I keep assuring him that the end of the book is not the end of our trips. As for me, I may never be able to absorb all the emotions and experiences accumulated during these travels, but be that as it may, it is overcome by the pleasure of the memories. We both feel sure we will soon return to many of these falls we've come to love. ■

Listen!
The sound of the
Wind in a million trees
Is held as a captive within
The falls

Trees at Mill Pond Falls

Bunchberries near Lower Tahquamenon Falls   110

ymeadow Falls

Upper Tahquamenon Falls

ower Tahquamenon Falls

Rock near Upper Tahquamenon Falls; At right, Lower Tahquamenon Falls;
Following pages: p. 116, white cedar trees near Haymeadow Falls; p. 118, Ocqueoc Falls; p. 119, tree near Ocqueoc Falls

114

We are
The sentinals
Of a once great army
Waging a desperate battle
With man.
Our great
Fear is that man,
In all his infinite
Ignorance and stupidity,
Will win

*Roads are
To be followed,
Not for their endings but
For the joy and wonder of the
Going*

A wilderness road near Ocqueoc Falls

1. Saxon Falls
   Superior Falls
2. Gorge Falls
   Great Conglomerate Falls
   Potawatomi Falls
   Rainbow Falls
   Sandstone Falls
3. Gabbro Falls
4. Abinodji Falls
   Iagoo Falls
   Manabezho Falls
   Manido Falls
   Nawadaha Falls
   Nokomis Falls
   Ogima Falls
   Ogimakwe Falls
5. Greenstone Falls
   Overlooked Falls *
   Union Falls
6. Yondota Falls
7. Greenwood Falls
   Nonesuch Falls
8. Kakabika Falls
9. Agate Falls
   Bond Falls
10. Sturgeon River Gorge Falls
11. Tibbets Falls
12. Eagle River Falls
    Jacobs Falls
13. Manganese Falls
    Silver River Falls
14. Haven Falls

15. Douglass Houghton Falls
    Hungarian Falls (3)
16. Falls River Falls (3)
17. Sturgeon Canyon Falls
18. Daults Falls
    Silver Falls
19. Black Slate Falls *
    Quartzite Falls *
    Slate River Falls
20. Big Eric's Falls
    Erik's Falls
21. Alder Falls
22. Black River Falls
23. Warner Falls *
24. Frohling Falls
25. Laughing Whitefish Falls
    Rock River Falls
26. Au Train Falls
27. Scott Falls
28. Alger Falls
    Munising Falls
    Wagner Falls
29. Miner's Falls
    Chapel Falls
30. Sable Falls
31. Upper Tahquamenon Falls
32. Lower Tahquamenon Falls
33. Haymeadow Falls
34. Mill Pond Falls *
35. Fumee Falls
36. Ocqueoc Falls

* Falls not named on the maps, named by the Elfonts.

I have been asked many times why I chose to photograph Michigan's waterfalls in black and white rather than color. My answer has always been that, for me, color takes away from the essence of an image. Black and white allows form, shape, and mood to surface without superficial distractions. The photographer who chooses to use black and white for landscape and still life work becomes acutely aware of the need to avoid distractions, and so his focus becomes influenced by what I refer to as "light isolates." These are the major elements in a scene or view that provide the emotional impact. The surrounding environment acts as supporting elements for these isolates. A light isolate may be a single unit or combination of units, and the photographer must continually be aware of how light separates these units from their surroundings. The quality of light therefore, becomes the governing factor in whether a subject projects something positive within the scene, or blends into its surroundings without meaning. It is the responsibility of the photographer to eliminate any distractions so that the light isolate becomes the most important element in the viewfinder or ground glass. Accomplishing this is not always as easy as it may sound. The successful black and white photographer learns to develop a monochromatic thought process. Visualization of the scene is done in shades of grey, not in colors. The photographs in this book were taken with the aforementioned philosophy as a basic tenant.

A full tonal scale in the final image was achieved by adhering to the old adage expose for the shadows and develop for the highlights. Many of you will recognize this as the fundamental principle in Zone System photography. There are many publications that treat this subject in detail, so I won't attempt to deal with it here. For those who are interested, I would recommend Ansel Adam's Basic Photo Series or Minor White's Zone System Manual.

The equipment I chose for this assignment was all large format with the exception of our last trip when I also used a Hasselblad 2 square camera. The large format cameras used were a Deardorf 8x10 field camera and a Cambo SCII 4x5 monorail camera. Both require the use of a dark cloth and the image is viewed and focused on a ground glass back. A variety of lenses, from 90 millimeters to 600 millimeters, were included in my gear. I selected a lens based on my position in relation to the subject, keeping in mind those areas I wished to include or eliminate from the final image. This gave me negatives that, with few exceptions, required no cropping and could be printed edge to edge in their entirety.

My film selection included Ilford HP4 (now designated HP5), Kodak Tri X, Kodak Technical Pan 2415, and for the Hasselblad, Agfa 100. The HP4 and Tri X were rated at ASA 250, the Technical Pan at 32, and the Agfa 100 at 80. These films gave me the range of speeds with which I am most comfortable when photographing landscapes and still life. I have always tried to capture the

Common Mullein at Yondota Falls

dynamic nature of waterfalls. This requires the use of slow shutter speeds which makes a tripod and cable release essential to assure the stability of the camera during exposure. I prefer small apertures which increase depth of field. Technical data on each exposure is listed on the following pages.

All metering was done with a Pentax digital spot meter. Film was developed in Kodak HC110 or Agfa Rodinal. Finished images were printed on Agfa Portriga Rapid paper using either Dupont 54D or Variotone developer.

I have photographed many waterfalls, both before and since the work for this book was completed. They have given me much enjoyment, perhaps because of their dynamic nature, perhaps because of their therapeutic effect on my psyche. However, I haven't felt the need to dissect my emotional response to them. That they provide me with pleasureable sensations, both in the seeing and the seeking, is enough to keep me going back to old falls, and searching out new ones.

CHAPTER I

2. Au Train Falls, Alger County
   12" Turner-Reich lens, ½ sec. f/22, 8x10 format, HP4 film

11. Gabbro Falls, Gogebic County
   25" Turner-Reich lens, 1/5 sec. f/45, 5x7 format, HP4 film

16. Superior Falls, Gogebic County
   150mm Symmar S lens, 5 secs. f/45,
   4x5 format, Technical Pan film

20. Manabezho Falls, Gogebic County
   19" Turner-Reich lens, ½ sec. f/45, 8x10 format, HP4 film

24. Saxon Falls, Gogebic County
   150mm Symmar S lens, 5 secs. f/45,
   4x5 format, Technical Pan film

25. Saxon Falls, Gogebic County
   18½" Kodak Anastigmat lens, 5 secs. f/64,
   4x5 format, Technical Pan film

26. Pine Trees At Overlooked Falls, Ontonagon County
   210mm Symmar lens, 2 mins. f/45,
   4x5 format, Technical Pan film

27. Overlooked Falls, Ontonagon County
   210mm Symmar lens, 10 secs. f/32, 4x5 format, HP4 film

28. Manido Falls, Gogebic County
   7¼" Dagor lens, ½ sec. f/16, green filter,
   8x10 format, HP4 film

29. Rocks At Manido Falls, Gogebic County
   14" Red Dot Artar lens, 5 secs. f/45, 8x10 format, HP4 film

30. Rock Patterns At Greenwood Falls, Ontonagon County
   19" Turner-Reich lens, 3 secs. f/64, polarizing filter,
   8x10 format, HP4 film

32. Bond Falls, Ontonagon County
   25" Turner-Reich lens, 3 secs. f/45, 5x7 format, HP4 film

33. Bond Falls, Ontonagon County
   7¼" Dagor lens, 1/5 sec. f/22, 8x10 format, HP4 film

34.-35. Agate Falls, Ontonagon County
   14" Red Dot Artar lens, ½ sec. f/22, 8x10 format, HP4 film

CHAPTER II

41. Upper Hungarian Falls, Houghton County
   7¼" Dagor lens, 1/5 sec. f/45, 4x5 format, HP4 film

42. Middle Hungarian Falls, Houghton County
   12" Turner-Reich lens, 5 sec. f/32, 8x10 format, HP4 film

43. Young Girl At Middle Hungarian Falls, Houghton County
   210mm Symmar lens, 1/5 sec. f/22, 4x5 format, HP4 film

44. Eagle River Falls, Keweenaw County
   150mm Symmar S lens, 1/15 sec. f/45, 4x5 format, HP4 film

45. Jacob's Falls, Keweenaw County
   7¼" Dagor lens, 1/5 sec. f/45, 4x5 format, HP4 film

46. Silver River Falls, Keweenaw County
   7¼" Dagor lens, 1/5 sec. f/32, 4x5 format, Technical Pan film

47. Haven Falls, Keweenaw County
   7¼" Dagor lens, 1/5 sec. f/45, 4x5 format, HP4 film

48.-49. Lake Fanny Hooe, Keweenaw County
   18½" Kodak Anastigmat Process Lens, 3½ min.
   f/64, 4x5 format, Technical Pan film

CHAPTER III

54. Sturgeon River Gorge Falls, Houghton County
   12" Turner-Reich lens, 5 sec. f/45, 8x10 format, HP4 film

59. Upper Falls, Falls River, Baraga County
   7¼" Dagor lens, ½ sec. f/22, 8x10 format, HP4 film

60. Upper Falls, Falls River, Baraga County
   7¼" Dagor lens, 3 sec. f/32, 8x10 format, HP4 film

61. Middle Falls, Falls River, Baraga County
   12" Turner-Reich lens, ½ sec. f/22, 8x10 format, HP4 film

62. Lower Falls, Falls River, Baraga County
   14" Red Dot Artar lens, ½ sec. f/32, 8x10 format, HP4 film

63. Silver Falls, Baraga County
   12" Turner-Reich lens, 5 sec. f/32, 8x10 format, HP4 film

64. Birch Tree At Sturgeon River Gorge, Southern Houghton County
   14" Red Dot Artar lens, 1 sec. f/45, 4x5 format, Tri X film

65. Birch Trees At Sturgeon River Gorge, Southern Houghton County
   14" Red Dot Artar lens, 1 sec. f/16, orange filter,
   4x5 format, Tri X film

66. Slate Formations At Slate River Falls, Baraga County
   25" Turner-Reich lens, 10 sec. f/16, 8x10 format, HP4 film

67. Slate River Falls, Baraga County
   14" Red Dot Artar lens, 3½ min. f/22, 5x7 format, HP4 film

68. Slate River Falls, Baraga County
   12" Turner-Reich lens, 5 sec. f/16, 8x10 format, HP4 film

69. Marsh Near Sturgeon River Gorge, Houghton County
   210mm. Symmar Lens, ½ sec. f/45, orange filter,
   4x5 format, Tri X film

70. Black Slate Falls, Baraga County
   7¼" Dagor lens, ½ sec. f/45, 4x5 format, Technical Pan film

71. Quartzite Falls, Baraga County
   14" Red Dot Artar lens, 1 sec. f/45, 4x5 format,
   Technical Pan film

72. Rock Patterns At Erik's Falls, Baraga County
   18½" Turner-Reich lens, 1 min. f/45, 5x7 format, HP4 film

73. Erik's Falls, Baraga County
   14" Red Dot Artar lens, 1/10 sec. f/32, 8x10 format, HP4 film

74.-75. Black Slate Falls, Baraga County
   12" Turner-Reich lens, 7 sec. f/45, 8x10 format, HP4 film

CHAPTER IV

81. Black River Falls, Marquette County
   210mm Symmar lens, ½ sec. f/45,
   4x5 format, Technical Pan film

82. Laughing Whitefish Falls, Alger County
7¼" Dagor lens, 2 sec. f/32, 4x5 film, HP4 film

86. Birch Tree Near Black River Falls, Marquette County
25" Turner-Reich lens, 1 sec. f/32, 5x7 format, HP4 film

88. Birch Trees Near Alder Falls, Marquette County
18½" Kodak Anastigmat Process lens, 12 sec. f/64,
4x5 format, Technical Pan film

89. Alger Falls, Alger County
210mm Symmar lens, 1 sec. f/45, 4x5 format, Technical Pan film

90. Warner Creek Falls, Marquette County
14" Red Dot Artar lens, ½ sec. f/32,
4x5 format, Technical Pan film

91. Frohling Falls, Marquette County
150mm Symmar S lens, 15 sec. f/32,
4x5 format, Technical Pan film

92. Ferns Near Rock River Falls, Alger County
210mm Symmar lens, 1/5 sec. f/45, orange filter,
4x5 film, Tri X film

93. Rock River Falls, Alger County
7¼" Dagor lens, 1/5 sec. f/32, yellow filter,
4x5 format, Tri X film

94. Wagner Falls, Alger County
12" Turner-Reich lens, 1 min. f/32, 8x10 format, HP4 film

95. Scott Falls, Alger County
7¼" Dagor lens, 5 sec. f/22, 8x10 format, HP4 film

96. Miner's Falls, Alger County
14" Red Dot Artar lens, ½ sec. f/22, 8x10 format, HP4 film

97. Reeds And Reflections, Alger County
18½" Kodak Anastigmat Process lens, 1 min. f/45,
4x5 format, Technical Pan film

98. Pine Tree Graveyard Near Chapel Falls, Alger County
14" Red Dot Artar lens, ½ sec. f/64, orange filter,
4x5 format, Technical Pan film

99. Chapel Falls, Alger County
14" Red Dot Artar lens, ¼ sec. f/22, 8x10 format, HP4 film

100. Alder Falls, Marquette County
7¼" Dagor lens, 4 sec. f/32, 4x5 format, Technical Pan film

101. Birch Trees Near Alder Falls, Marquette County
18½" Kodak Anastigmat Process lens, 12 sec. f/64,
4x5 format, Technical Pan film

CHAPTER V

107. Lower Fumee Falls, Dickinson County
7¼" Dagor lens, 1/3 sec. f/32, red filter, 4x5 format, HP4 film

108. Trees At Mill Pond Falls, Dickinson County
18½" Kodak Anastigmat Process lens, 3 sec f/64,
4x5 format, Technical Pan film

109. Mill Pond Falls, Dickinson County
210mm Symmar lens, 1/5 sec. f/45, 4x5 format, HP4 film

*110. Bunchberries Near Lower Tahquamenon Falls,
Chippewa County*
80mm Planar lens on Hasselblad, 10 sec. f/22,
2¼ sq. format, Agfa 100 film

111. Haymeadow Falls, Delta County
18½" Kodak Anastigmat Process lens, 5 sec. f/64,
4x5 format, HP4 film

112. Upper Tahquamenon Falls, Luce County
24" Apo Ronar lens, 3 sec. f/64, polarizing filter,
8x10 format, HP4 film

113. Lower Tahquamenon Falls, Chippewa County
18½" Kodak Anastigmat Process lens, 3 sec. f/64,
4x5 format, Technical Pan film

114. Rock Near Upper Tahquamenon Falls, Luce County
80mm Planar lens on Hasselblad, 10 sec. f/22,
2¼ sq. format, Agfa 100 film

115. Lower Tahquamenon Falls, Chippewa County
210mm Symmar lens, 1 sec. f/32, 4x5 format, Technical Pan film

116. White Cedar Trees Near Haymeadow Falls, Delta County
14" Red Dot Artar lens, 50 sec. f/45, 4x5 format, HP4 film

118. Ocqueoc Falls, Presque Isle County
20" Bausch and Lomb Process lens, 1/10 sec. f/45,
polarizing filter, 8x10 format, HP4 film

119. Trees Near Ocqueoc Falls, Presque Isle County
20" Bausch and Lomb Process lens, ½ sec. f/32,
8x10 format, HP4 film

120. Common Mullein Near Yondota Falls, Gogebic County
14" Red Dot Artar lens, 37 secs. f/64,
4x5 format, Technical Pan film

124. A Wilderness Road Near Ocqueoc Falls, Presque Isle County
80mm Planar lens on Hasselblad, 5 sec. f/22,
2¼ sq. format, Agfa 100 film

EQUIPMENT

Cameras
Deardorf 8x10 Field Camera with 8x10 and 5x7 backs
Cambo SCII monorail camera with 4x5 back
Hasselblad 500 CM

Lenses
90 mm Super Angulon
150 mm. Symar S
7" Dagor
210 mm. Symmar convertible
14" Red Dot Artar
14" Apo Ronar
18" Kodak Anastigmat Process
20" Bausch and Lomb Process
24" Apo Ronar Process
80 mm. Planar
150 mm. Sonnar
Turner-Reich Triple Convertible

Meter
Pentax digital spotmeter

Tripods
Slik Master Pro II
Gitzo Sport Gilux with −2 head

I N D E X